CADET GRAY & BUTTERNUT BROWN

Notes on the Confederate Uniforms

by Thomas M. Arliskas

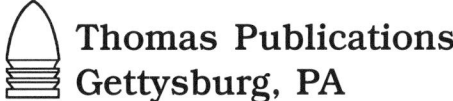

Thomas Publications
Gettysburg, PA

To my father and mother,

Bill and Betty Arliskas.

Copyright © 2006 Thomas M. Arliskas

Printed and bound in the United States of America

Published by THOMAS PUBLICATIONS
  P.O. Box 3031
  Gettysburg, Pa. 17325

All rights reserved. No part of this book may be used or reproduced without written permission of the author and the publisher, except in the case of brief quotations embodied in critical essays and reviews.

ISBN-1-57747-122-9

Front cover illustration, a portion of "Men of Arkansas," painting by Don Troiani, *www.historicalartprints.com*

Contents

Acknowledgements 4

An Introduction to Confederate Military Clothing 5

Chapter 1   Early War Period, 1861 – October 1862
    Part One   Volunteers at all times, are to provide their own clothing, and receive
                        accumulation in money 8
    Part Two   Each man was to get just what suited his fancy 12
    Part Three   Never has there been a more patriotic people than ours! 18
    Part Four   Poor soldiers, how you you are imposed upon 23
    Part Five   They looked like all the rest, a motley looking set of men in their
                        various uniforms 27
    Part Six   The loss of public property has been great, and cannot be replaced 34
    Part Seven It is a sad parcel of soldiers here, who are now naked and barefoot 39
    Part Eight   There were so many varieties of dress...they could scarcely be said to
                        have a uniform 42

Chapter 2   Middle War Period, October 1862 – November 1864
    Part One   The Quartermaster's Lament 50
    Part Two   They were generally well dressed as far as comfort was concerned, but
                        didn't present a very military appearance 55
    Part Three   Neat uniforms of gray jackets and trousers of light blue 58
    Part Four   We were not all entirely dressed in gray uniforms 62
    Part Five   Well clad and armed, tolerably well shod 66
    Part Six   An Officer's uniform out here costs three-hundred and fifty dollars and
                        it's impossible to get a good one 70
    Part Seven A panic which I never before witnessed, seemed to have seized on both
                        officers and men 72
    Part Eight   The Depots are quite bare 74
    Part Nine   Greater suffering and privation than anything experienced...during the
                        whole struggle 76
    Part Ten   Those serving in Northern Virginia and the mountainous district should
                        be preferred 77
    Part Eleven In nearly all the branches of supply...we are not yet exempt from dependence
                        on foreign importation 80

Chapter 3   Late War Period, November 1864 – April 1865
    Part One   The demand for shoes will soon be greater than ever 82
    Part Two   Clothing was sparsely issued.... Shoes were scarce. I do not remember
                        the issue of a single overcoat, and but a few blankets 86
    Part Three   The Army pay is in arrears for several months. This is an excuse for desertion,
                        the sale of clothing, equipments and ammunitions by the soldiers 88
    Part Four   We turned and scorched the seams of our underwear on account of insects,
                        we had no way of boiling our clothing 90
    Part Five   They were wearied, earnest looking men, wearing butternut and gray
                        colored clothing and broad-brimmed hats 95

Endnotes 99

Acknowledgements.

I want to thank everyone, my wife Terry, my family, and my friends for encouraging me to finish this book.

I have talked to hundreds of people over the last fifteen years and if I forgot anyone's name, please forgive me, and you're free to remind me of it later.

Most notable contributors are Frederick P. Todd who was my mentor years ago, Mike McAfee, Dick Pielen, Dick Tibbals, Bob Parker, Lee White, John Hennessy, Mark Hubbs, Ron Field, Ross Brooks, Les Jensen, Jerry Coates, Bill Adams, Bob Huntoon, Howie Madaus, Charlie Childs, Rick Simmons and Family and Geoff Waldren, who all shared their enthusiasm and time with me.

Thanks to the noted Civil War authors, Wiley Sword, Pete Cozzens, Phil Katcher, and Chris Calkins, who shared notes and permission to quote from their works. A special thanks to Don Troiani who also shared some time and words with me on Confederate uniforms.

Special thanks to collectors Jeffrey N. Brown, Herb Peck Jr., Jim Brinks, Tom Molacea, Leighton Young, Kenneth Dennen and Emory Morgan who shared their photos with me, many of which are printed in this book. To my buddies Chuck Foster and Mike Collins, and all the guys on the 15th Tennessee, and my NSSA team who pushed me, sometimes too hard!

And to all the people at the Springfield Historical Society and the Plainfield Public Library in Illinois, who put up with me for all those years. To Peter Harrington, curator of the Anne S. K. Brown Military Collection, Brown University Library, my special thanks. And I cannot not forget my friends Mike Winey and Randy Hackenberg of the U. S. Army Military History Institute, Special Collections Archives, Carlisle Barracks, in Pennsylvania, who shared their time and expertise with a strange man who likes to study Confederate uniforms.

Since I started researching, several excellent works and articles on Confederate uniforms have been published. Some stole a bit of my thunder, and although disappointed at not being the first to present something, I felt I was on the right track. If two or three authors arrive at the same conclusions, there is a good chance those conclusions are correct.

For the record, the one thing I know for sure about Confederate uniforms is how much I do not know! This statement is not a disclaimer, just reality.

This work is a collection of notes I have accumulated, and is not intended as the last word on Confederate uniforms. This research will be an ongoing endeavor.

To all of you with an interest in this subject, Confederate uniform history has to be built one step, or brick, at a time. Hopefully, this book is a step in that direction, or a brick if you prefer.

Tom Arliskas.

An Introduction to Confederate Military Clothing of the American Civil War

Near Waldron, North Carolina, May 11, 1861, a month after the commencement of the Civil War, April 12, 1861:

> The 2nd North Carolina troops stationed at this point...have no arms, and most of their uniforms, if they may be so-called, are as varied as their faces. Some of the officers wear red flannel sashes and yellow flannel epaulettes. A few mount the French chapeau, and now and then, a full dressed individual relieves the general monotony of the [common] homespun.

After the surrender of Fort Donelson near Dover, Tennessee, in February 1862, the men of the captured 14th Mississippi Infantry mingled with Federal soldiers who commented on their clothing:

> They looked like all the rest, a motley looking set of men in various uniforms. I saw one or two regiments who wore blankets made of pieces of carpeting.

A field editor for the *Memphis Daily Appeal*, on assignment with the Confederate Army of Mississippi in September 1862, described for its readers one of the more famous regiments in Confederate service, Terry's Texas Rangers of the 8th Texas Cavalry:

> They were shabby, dirty, ragged, and try to clothe themselves as best they can. The only badge they wore was a red star on the front of their hats or caps. One of them had a whole suit of bearskins, and several have pants of the same material. They are armed with short double-barreled shotguns, revolvers, and Bowie knives.

Back east in Virginia, Branch's North Carolina Brigade, after the Battle of Hanover Courthouse in May 1862, presented an un-uniform appearance:

> Some were wrapped in blankets of rag carpet, others wore shoes of untanned hide. Others were without shoes or jackets and their heads were bound with handkerchiefs. Some in red shirts, some in stiff beaver hats, some were attired in shreds and patches of cloth, and a few wore the soiled garments of civilian gentleman. The mass adhered to homespun suits of gray or butternut, and the coarse blue kersey common to slaves. In places I caught glimpses of red zouave breeches or leggings, blue Federal caps, Federal buttons, and Federal blouses.

At the Battle of Gettysburg, Pennsylvania, July 1-3, 1863, a Federal soldier noted the dress of Lee's soldiers:

> The Confederates were dressed in gray and butternut, and wore for the most part, a slouch hat, a short jacket, and a blanket strapped over their shoulder and under their arm.

Private S. A. Hale of the 7th Arkansas Infantry described how he was uniformed at one point in the war:

> A broad brimmed flop hat, a good pair of Federal infantry shoes, some home made yarn socks, a pair of trousers to large in girth, and exceedingly short of leg, a shirt made out of piano cover of flax or hemp, with large red figures or cornucopias, and the body color like the old women's china.

At the Battle of Kelly's Ford in November 1863, members of Hay's Louisiana Brigade shocked their Yankee captors with fine new uniforms:

> The prisoners taken here were better clothed than any we had seen before. All were provided with overcoats and jackets or a much better material than our own. They were of English manufacture, much darker than the United States uniform, and this furnished conclusive evidence of successful blockade running.

The colors and fabrics in these contemporary descriptions go from bearskin suits to gray and brown homespun, to fine English imported wool jackets and overcoats. The variety in dress stimulates the imagination, but to many may seem odd or strange. Confederate soldiers wearing blue slave cloth, carpet blankets, and shirts from old piano covers is not the typical cadet gray clad, "Johnny Reb" the general public identifies with in movies and paintings.

New research is being done on the Confederate Provisional Army, their uniforms, accoutrements, and firearms that will change forever our perceptions of what type of clothing and uniforms were actually worn by the armies of the Southern Confederacy.

If ever there was a historical question posed by artists, authors, collectors, and Civil War living historians, it is how were the Confederates uniformed at the battles of Shiloh, Sharpsburg, Gettysburg or Atlanta? Were they all in gray uniforms? Were they all uniformed alike or differently dressed? Some will answer, "They wore anything," and while partially true, research shows whole brigades dressed in the same uniform at different times during the war.

The material that is available on clothing or uniforms is usually found in one sentence or one-paragraph descriptions. Confederate quartermaster documents give us the numbers issued but usually no color or type given. All these bits of information must be put into some type of order or sequence. As an aid, the study of Confederate clothing can be divided into three-time spans or periods, early, middle, and late war.

The early period runs from 1859, the year of John Brown's raid into Harpers Ferry, Virginia, to incite a slave rebellion, which led to the creation of hundreds of Southern militia companies, to October 1862, when the Confederate armies were reported naked and barefoot, ending the Commutation Law. Under the Commutation Law of May 1861, each Confederate soldier was paid a yearly sum for providing himself a uniform.

The early war period was the most colorful phase of the war in terms of martial splendor, as each new state militia or volunteer company arrived for muster in a uniform of its own choice or design. Much of the uniform information we have is from the early period. The majority of the photographs of Confederate soldiers dates from the first year of the war when it was still a great adventure to be recorded in pictures and flowery Victorian prose. The variety seen was endless, but short-lived. By late summer of 1861, the shakos, white belts, plumes, and dress uniforms were sent home or put in storage. The volunteers, after four months of camp and field duty, had worn out their clothing. A force of over 200,000 men now had to be re-supplied for the coming winter, but from where?

The Confederate Quartermaster Department initially had contracted only for the uniforms of the Regular Army, not the volunteers. The volunteers had to supply themselves under the Commutation Law and received money to buy clothing. The Quartermaster made the statement that he could not make up or purchase enough clothing for everyone, and suggested getting it from overseas. The Confederate government, acting on a suggestion from some concerned citizens, appealed to the people instead, asking them to contribute warm winter clothing under the Great Appeal of August 1861. Patriotic donations became the most important supply source for the soldiers during the winter of 1861-62, and all through the following year.

By September 1862, after a long summer and fall of hard, active campaigning, both armies east and west were reported in rags, with many barefoot in the cold weather. As a result of seeing the victorious Confederate Army marching through Richmond in rags, and millions having been spent by the government for quartermaster goods, the Commutation Law was dropped as ineffective and the Quartermaster of the Confederacy made responsible for providing each soldier with a proper uniform. By the spring of 1863, the entire operation of the Quartermaster Department was completely redone and reorganized.

The middle war period runs from October 1862 to July 1864. This period brings the development of the Quartermaster Department. Under its direction the meager resources of the South were placed under departmental officers, and Quartermaster Depots, supply, shipping, and manufacturing centers, were set up all over the South. These centers were under the direct control of the Quartermaster General. Importation of military goods like cloth, shoes, uniforms, medicines, and ordnance, also came under stricter government control.

The Great Appeals, state donations, and the early operations of the Quartermaster Department all added to the diversity of uniforms we hear described as, "no two dressed alike." With the increased output of the different manufacturing depots in the South, whole regiments and brigades were receiving all new uniforms of the same style and color from government stocks. It was never enough, however, to satisfy every need and circumstance. By the winter of 1863-1864, supplies were again reported exhausted. Emergency methods were used, sending the men home for clothes under Special Orders. The new Quartermaster General Lawton redoubled his efforts to produce garments and shoes.

This ushers in the late war period of July 1864 to April 1865. The late war period is interesting as the actual issue numbers for uniform clothing were contained in a special report to the Confederate Congress. Records show that uniforms and shoes were dispensed in great quantities, yet diaries and letters of the period tell of ragged and barefooted soldiers all over again. The failed transportation system was responsible for the shortages. The Confederate rail system was wrecked or worn out, the seaports were being captured, and the wagons and horses in the last months of the war were in very short supply. The supplies and clothing were available, but getting it there was sometimes impossible.

Thus, it can be concluded that the Confederates used several sources of clothing. To accurately depict an early, middle, or late war period soldier by state, regiment, army, or department, takes some research.

Wearing a gray jacket or frock coat, gray or blue trousers, and an old battered hat and a rolled up blanket over the shoulder, is not the typical Confederate soldier of the years 1861-1865. A Confederate private's appearance changed month-to-month, winter-to-winter, and circumstance-to-circumstance. Each company or individual had their own story to tell, their own trials in keeping properly clothed. Some did better than others, usually through the hard work of their quartermaster officers or state governments, and some boasted they never took a piece of clothing from the Confederate government, trusting to the folks back home, or what was found on the battlefield.

The best any historian can do is to put the information he finds out there, hoping that others will help by augmenting it with their own findings. There are thousands of bits of information on Confederate uniform history in collections, historical societies, museums, libraries, that can all add to the current research. This book and others like it is a start in answering the question, "What did the Rebels really look like?"

Confederate prisoners, Chancellorsville, VA, 1863. LOC

CHAPTER 1

Early War Period, 1861 – October 1862

"Volunteers at all times, are to provide their own clothing, and receive accumulation in money."

— C. S. War Department, May 6, 1861

The study of Confederate Provisional and Regular Army clothing starts with the different Congressional Acts ratified by the newly formed Confederate Congress in February and March 1861. In these Acts are found the laws governing how the Provisional, Regular, and all Volunteer forces of the Confederacy were to be recruited, paid, and clothed while in their countries service.

On March 6, 1861, An Act to Provide for the Public Defense, and An Act For the Establishment and Organization of the Army of the Confederate States, were passed and signed into law. The state militias could be called out for service for six months if needed, and an all-volunteer army of 100,000 men was to be enrolled for a period of twelve months. A Confederate Regular Army of 10,000 was to be enlisted along with the volunteers.

Under Sections 3 and 4 of An Act to Provide for the Public Defense were the orders concerning how the men entering military service were to uniform themselves. They stated in part:

> that said volunteers shall furnish their own clothes... and instead of clothing, every non-commissioned officer and private in any company shall be entitled, when called into actual service, in money to a sum equal to the cost of clothing of a non-commissioned officer or private in the Regular Army of the Confederate States.

As an example, Governor Rector of Arkansas was asked to recruit one regiment of infantry for Confederate service in Virginia on April 23, 1861. Along with the terms and conditions of their regimental organization, in the section covering clothing, each Arkansas volunteer was told they were to "furnish their own uniforms, but would receive their value in accumulation."[1]

The actual dollar amount for this clothing was set on May 21, 1861, with a revision to the March 6 Act. A new Act, *Concerning the Transportation of Soldiers, an Allowance for Clothing of Volunteers, and Amendatory of the Act for the Establishment and Organization of the Army of the Confederate States*, informed the new recruits that under Section 2:

> There shall be allowed to each volunteer, to be paid him on the first muster and payroll after being received and mustered into the service of the Confederate States, the sum of $21.00, in lieu of clothing for six months, and thereafter the same allowance in money at every subsequent period of service for six months; PROVIDED, That the price of clothing in kind received by said volunteers from the Confederate States Government shall be deducted first from the money thus allowed.

The new Act seemed simple enough to understand. Each soldier was to be paid $21.00 for providing a uniform and $21.00 every six months thereafter for extra clothing while in this country's service. The acquisition of a new uniform for many soldiers was anything but simple. With no funds, and no source of supply for military clothing in the rural areas of the South, Richmond was their only choice. Typical is the request given by General T. C. Hindman to the new Confederate Secretary of War, L. P. Walker. In a letter to Walker, Hindman explained the inability of his home state Arkansas to equip the volunteers:

> [We] have no money. Can get it here [Helena, Arkansas if needed]. If ordered [to Fort Smith, Arkansas instead of Virginia], can't you send blankets for the men? Blue jeans for their shirts and pants and swords for the officers, and stop pay to cover the cost? All much needed. Can't get them here in the Southwest.[2]

Frederick William Bush,
Co. E., The Saline Guards,
1st Fagan's Arkansas Infantry.

Bush's uniform of battle shirt and black striped trousers is typical of the early war period. The shirts' actual colors are unknown, but gray shirt and black facings were popular with the 1st Arkansas. Bush's uniform has officer's shoulder straps, but from army records he never rose above the rank of sergeant. Bush survived the war and quietly passed away in Benton, Arkansas, in 1914. (USAMHI)

Walker answered all such requests by referring to the conditions of the commutation laws found in the March 6 Act. To hopefully put the matter to rest, a letter was addressed to the general public on May 6, 1861, restating the policy on who was to provide clothing. The following message appeared in several of the major Southern newspapers:

> Many volunteer companies, battalions, and regiments, entered the Confederate service with the idea the War Department would supply all the deficiencies of clothing among them, and would be prepared to meet the reoccurring wants of its soldiers, who are now suffering in this respect. Volunteers at all times, are to provide their clothing, and receive accumulation in money.[3]

Despite the efforts of the War Department to get out the message, many officers and men still did not know that such laws were in place. From a cavalryman in the 1st Virginia Regiment during the spring and summer of 1861, "the men did not dream they were to be paid anything. . .or the Government to clothe them. [We] bought our uniforms, and when these wore out, we ordered new ones from home."[4] This same individual, needing a new pair of boots, was told to see the Quartermaster. To the astonishment of the cavalryman, "the official refused my cash, contenting himself with deducting the amount from my pay and clothing allowance."[5]

A great joke spread through the camp of the 1st Virginia. If a soldier owed someone money, he would tell the injured party to go see the Quartermaster, and take it out of his "pay money account"!

Arthur P. Ford, of the 17th South Carolina Militia Regiment, Palmetto Guards, knew of the commutation law and explained it in his memoirs:

> At this [early] period of the War, the Confederate Government allowed each soldier a certain yearly sum for a uniform, and each company decided for itself what uniform it should be. In consequence, "uniform" was really an inappropriate term to apply to the various organizations.
>
> At first our company was uniformed in gray woolen frocks and trousers of the same material, with blue caps. Next we had gray cotton coats and trousers with gray cloth hats. Then very dark brown coats with blue trousers furnished by the Government, which assumed to provide also the hats, shoes, and underclothing. The shoes when we could get them were heavy English brogans, very hard on the feet, but durable.
>
> The summer of 1862 brought our first allowance for uniforms. The new uniforms, (at a price $2.00 over the allotment), was a very inferior half cotton, half wool which served us to the end of the year.[6]

Another revision to the commutation law came in August 1861. Questions concerning to whom the commutation monies were to be paid, how much, and for what articles were spelled out for the parties involved. In a letter to the Army, Acting Secretary of War Judah P. Benjamin wrote the following:

✦ Early War Period, 1861 – October 1862 ✦

IN RELATION TO CLOTHING FOR VOLUNTEERS UNDER ACT OF 8TH AUGUST, 1861.

1. Whereas any State shall furnish to its troops and volunteers in the Confederate service, the clothing required according to the regulations of the Department, payment thereafter will be made at the commutation rate of twenty-five dollars every six months, on receipts produced by the State to be signed by the commanding officer, as the case may be, certifying the number of men actually furnished by the State.
2. Whenever any State or the commander of any volunteer company shall furnish to the volunteers a portion only of the clothing required by the regulations, payment for the same will be made on the receipt above mentioned, on the following basis viz, a calculation will be made of the sum necessary to supply the articles deficient at the rates established by Quartermaster Department Bureau. This sum will be deducted from the commutation money, and the remainder paid to the State or commander as the case may be, as being the money value of the portion furnished by such State or commander.
3. The 77th paragraph of the regulations for the Quartermaster Bureau, as adopted by this Department, show what quantity and articles of clothing are required to be provided for each soldier.

Per 77th — a Soldier is allowed clothing stated in the following table or articles thereof of equal value. When a balance is due him at the end of the year, it is added to his allowance for the next.

Clothing	1st Yr.	2nd Yr.	3rd Yr.
Cap, complete	2	1	1
Cover	1	1	1
Coat	2	1	1
Trowsers	3	2	2
Flannel Shirts	3	3	3
Bootees	4	4	4
Flannel drawers	3	2	2
Leather stock	1	—	—
Great Coat	1	—	—
Stable frock (mounted men)	1	—	—
Fatigue overalls (for engineers and ordnance)	1	1	11
Blanket	1	—	1

Mounted men may receive one pair of boots and two pair of bootees instead of four pairs of bootees. The allowance for clothing is only for such as is furnished to the volunteers subsequent to their being accepted into service by the Government. The Government has made the provisions for reimbursing to the soldier the value of the clothing that he has when he entered the service.[7]

A letter from the Quartermaster General, May 26, 1861.

Despite all the efforts of the War Department, Acting Quartermaster General Abraham C. Myers was still receiving requests for uniforms, tents, cash, and equipments almost daily in Richmond. His response to Col. Churchill, Knoxville, Tennessee, is courteous and to the point:

Sir;

The allowance of clothing money to each volunteer is $21, the first payment after being mustered into service and at the subsequent periods of six months. To make this available for clothing volunteers a regulation is made to the following effect. The person furnishing the clothing may obtain his pay by presenting to the paying officer the receipt of the Volunteer, verified by the certificate of his Company Commander, provided the amount does not exceed $21. If the volunteer provides himself [a uniform], he draws the allowance or such part of it as may not be assigned to a furnisher.

The Army regulations are not printed; those of the U. S. Army you are referred to until ours come from the printer.

The pay of an infantry private of Volunteers is $11 per month, and private of cavalry $12.

If you will send to Jackson, Mississippi, you can procure canvas for tents. They cannot be issued to you until your Regiment is mustered into service.

(Signed) A. C. Myers, A. Q. M. Gen'l

(N.A.R.A. Q. M. Letter Book)

Private Ford,
Palmetto Guard,
Co. A., 1st South Carolina Siege Artillery.

Private Ford described the uniform purchased by his company as, "gray frock coats and trousers of the same material, with blue caps." The Palmetto Guard were well clothed by C. S. standards. Confederate soldiers in other parts of the Confederacy were reduced to rags by the late summer of 1861.

Judah P. Benjamin,
Secretary of War of the Confederate States.

His peers thought him brilliant, and an exceptional lawyer, Harvard Class of 1828. Benjamin as Attorney General of the Confederate States, and later as Secretary of War, was instrumental in seeing the early volunteers properly clothed. Under the first Great Appeal of 1861, Benjamin made the statement, "*Clothing need not be as uniform to be excepted. Anything to keep a man warm and clothed could be sent in.*" Over three million dollars in clothing came to the armies of the Confederacy under this governmentsponsored drive.

Andrew J. Freeze,
Co. B., 1st Virginia Cavalry.

With the appointment of Major J.E.B. Stuart as colonel in July 1861, and their dashing charge at the Battle of Bull Run against Ellworth's Fire Zouaves, the 1st Virginia became one of the famous Confederate regiments of the Civil War. Freeze's early war photo shows him in gray frock coat with yellow or gold braiding on the chest. By the fall of 1862, his regiment was described as wearing, "light drab gray or butternut…light jacket and trousers with black facings, the court costume of the regiment." (USAMHI)

❖ Early War Period, 1861 – October 1862 ❖

As the bureaus in Richmond worked to sort out the details of the commutation law, the soldiers continued to uniform themselves as best they could.

City or County Aid Societies or Military Sewing Circles made up the first uniform for many Confederate volunteers. The cloth was usually donated, the men were measured and patterns made and material cut out by the local tailor then given to the ladies to sew. As many companies as there were in service in April and May of 1861, each was in a different style of clothing or uniform. This includes the uniformed militia companies of the different Confederate States. By the fall of 1861, it was hoped that a standard uniform would replace the mix seen in the ranks. It would take another two years before the Quartermaster Department could comply. In the interim, just keeping the men warmly dressed was a task many officers found as hard to do as fighting the Yankees.

This clipping originally found in the *Montgomery (Alabama) Advertiser*, was reprinted in the *Columbus Daily Enquirer* for May 5, 1861. It explains to the public and the new volunteers of the Confederate Provisional Army that they, not the government in Richmond, were to provide their own clothing and receive reimbursement (commutation) for them.

"Each man was to get just what suited his fancy."

— Jno. W. Stewart, Co. K., 5th Texas Infantry.

The new volunteer companies were ordered to provide their own uniforms. The decision of type or style of uniform to adopt was next. What turned out to be an unofficial set of C.S. uniform regulations began to appear in several Southern papers in late May 1861. These were printed as an aid to those companies or private concerns making up uniforms for the new soldiers. These particular regulations were released to the public without approval of the War Department, and differed in several details with the forthcoming official regulations.

The unofficial set was brought to New Orleans by a local tailor and merchant, one Mr. Cain. Mr. Cain was one of several people who had been invited to Montgomery, Alabama, in February 1861, to help design a uniform for the Confederate Army. One source stated that over twenty different styles were submitted to the War Department, most of them based on European armies. The Committee apparently liked Mr. Cain's designs, or maybe he had taken some notes at the meetings; either way Cain gave the newspapers what became known at that time as the Confederate Army Uniform.[1]

A copy of these regulations was printed in the June 13 edition of the *Cairo Gazette*, an Illinois newspaper. It was put there for the benefit of the Union soldiers who were occupying Cairo to help them, "recognize their enemies."

How the Rebel Army Is Uniformed

The following is a description of the uniform adopted by Jeff Davis & Company for the equipment of the rebel army:

COAT — Short tunic of cadet gray, double breasted with two rows of buttons over the breast. The rows two inches apart at the waist and widening toward the shoulders. Suitable for cavalry as well as infantry.

PANTALOONS — Of sky blue cloth, made full in the leg, and trimmed according to corps - with blue for infantry, red for artillery, and yellow for cavalry, no other distinction.

For the Generals and officers of his staff, the dress will be of dark blue cloth, trimmed with gold; for the medical department black cloth, with gold and velvet trimmings.

All badges of distinction are to be marked upon the sleeves and collars. Badges of distinguished rank on the collars only. For a brigadier-general, three large stars; for a colonel, two large stars; for a lieutenant-colonel, one large star; for a major, one small star and horizontal bar; for captain, three small stars; for a first lieutenant, two small stars; for a second lieutenant, one small star.

A second set containing descriptions of military buttons appeared in the *New Orleans Daily Picayune*. Of the two, the *Picayune* copy was most often reprinted in the Southern papers.

Uniform of the Confederate States Army

We learn that the army regulations have been issued for the uniform adopted by the War Department of the Confederacy and are as follows: the coat to be of cadet gray cloth, short tunic, double breasted, two rows of buttons down the breast, two inches apart at the waist, and widening towards the shoulders.

Pantaloons of sky blue cloth, made full in the leg. The different corps of the service to be distinguished by the color of their trimmings — blue for infantry, red for artillery, and yellow for cavalry. The buttons to be of plain gilt, convex form, three quarters of an inch in diameter. In the artillery corps, the buttons to be stamped with the

---

From the letter book of Acting Q. M. Gen'l Myers to J. M. Gault, Assistant Q.M., New Orleans. Letter dated May 23, 1861, detailing the uniform at present adopted by the Confederate Army.

Colonel Myers desires me to enquire of you if his Department can purchase any blankets suitable for soldiers at the penitentiary, and if it is possible to obtain any clothing from the same source.

The coat of all enlisted men is double-breasted tunic, of cadet gray cloth, skirt to extend half-way between hip and knee, two rows of buttons on the breast, seven in each, distance between rows 4 inches at top and 3 at bottom; stand up collar to rise no higher than to permit the chin to turn freely over it to hook in front at bottom and slope thence backwards 30 degrees. Cuffs 2 ½ inches deep at under seam to button with two small buttons and be slightly pointed at upper part of arm pockets in fold of skirt, collars and cuffs to be of a color prescribed for facings of several corps, say light blue for such as you might have manufactured, the edges of the tunic to be trimmed throughout with the same color, narrow lining of gray material in the skirts of the tunic. The button for infantry is gilt, convex, plain with large raised letter center "I", small buttons ½ inch in diameter. If these cannot be obtained, any bright button might be used for the present.

The uniform trousers are to be of sky blue, <u>but in our need gray may be used</u>, they are to be loose, and to spread well over the foot.

The overcoat for footmen is of the same cloth, stand up collar, double-breasted cape extending to the elbow, when the arm is straight, to button all the way.

A blouse is allowed of light gray cloth, double-breasted, two rows of buttons; seven in each row, small turnover collar. Large orders will be given to any responsible person who will undertake to furnish such articles.

Colonel Myers suggests that if you are too much occupied the gentleman to whom you refer in your letter may give it attention.

(Signed) Larkin Smith, Major & A. Q. M.

A Confederate soldier wearing a uniform described in the first unofficial regulations. The frock coat has no facing colors or piping, is double-breasted, and only the trousers are faced in branch of service colors. USAMHI

❖ Early War Period, 1861 – October 1862 ❖

letter A, and the infantry and cavalry, the buttons will bear only the number of the regiment.

For the Generals and officers of his staff the dress will be of dark blue cloth, trimmed with gold, for the medical department, black cloth, and gold and velvet trimming. All badges of distinction were to be marked upon the sleeves and collars. Badges of distinguished rank on the collars only. For a Brigadier-General, three large stars; for a Colonel, two large stars; for a lieutenant-colonel, one large star; for a major, one small star, and a horizontal bar; for a Captain, three small stars, for a First Lieutenant, two small stars; for a Second Lieutenant, one small star.

For a General and staff officers the buttons will be of bright gilt, convex, rounded at the edge — a raised eagle at the center, surrounded by thirteen stars. Exterior diameter of large size buttons, 1 inch; of small size, 1/2 inch. For officers of the corps of engineers the same button is to be used, except in the place of the eagle and stars, will be a raised E in German text. For officers of artillery, infantry, rifleman, and cavalry, the button will be a plain gilt convex, with a large raised letter in the center - A for artillery, I for infantry, etc. The exterior diameter of large size buttons, 7/8 of an inch, small button 1/2 inch.

No cap has been adopted.[2]

The official *Confederate Uniform and Dress of the Army* regulations were issued out of Richmond under General Order No. 9. dated June 6, 1861. Many items were amended and a more detailed description given in the new regulations covering tunics, buttons, hats, spurs, gloves, sword belts, and overcoats.

The collars and cuffs of the enlisted man's tunic were now to be faced in the proper branch of service color, and the edges of the tunic to be trimmed throughout with the same colored cloth.[3]

A forage cap, modeled after the French Army kepi, was to be the official headgear for both officers and enlisted men, but color was not specified other than a model that was on display in the Quartermaster General's office.[4]

The most important change, and one set of regulations that were strictly adhered to, was that of officers' uniforms. The base color of the tunic was officially designated as cadet gray, and dark blue was dropped. The patterns for distinguishing rank were also modified to a new system of stars and bars on the collar, and an Austrian style braid to be placed on the sleeve.[5]

Pantaloons for field officers were to be light blue, the General staff retaining their dark blue color.[6]

A new button was to be worn by enlisted men in the infantry and all other branches of service. It was to contain the regimental number in the center. The artillery would keep their letter A for tunic buttons.[7]

These new regulations intended for the Confederate Regular Army of 10,000 men now became the uniform of the Provisional Army. A few of the volunteers did adopt the new regulations, but the majority of soldiers in the Army were unable to do so. For the Confederate government in Richmond to produce 200,000 new regulation uniforms in a short period of time was an impossible task in 1861, and even in 1862. Finances, cloth shortages, industrial capacity, and the commutation law made these regulations a dead letter. The closest many would ever get to the official uniform was the wearing of something gray in color.

The June 6 regulations arrived three months too late for most C. S. units who had already selected a uniform. Many wore instead a uniform chosen by their state Army Board, or one designed for their company. Having to provide their own clothing under the commutation law, and using an unofficial set of uniform regulations without illustrations, are some of the reasons for the great diversity seen in C. S. uniforms in 1861.

The situation was so confusing out in the camps that one soldier, upon asking why all the different clothing, was given the excuse by an officer that, "the regulations do not require a standard uniform."[8]

A Texas volunteer remembered when his company began to form that, "Just here someone suggested we have a uniform, no one knew what uniform meant, but we all were inclined to the idea...each man to get just what suited his fancy and have it made up in any style he chose — Jes' so it was uniform!"[9]

The English correspondent Charles Russell was anything but complimentary when describing these early war South Carolina volunteers in Charleston in April 1861:

> There is an endless variety, often ugliness, in dress and equipment and nomenclature among these companies. The headdress is generally, however, a smart cap like the French kepi; the tunic of different cuts, colors, facings, and materials green with gray and yellow facings, gray with orange and black and white, blue with white and yellow, roan, brown, burnt sienna, and olive jackets, frocks, tunics, blouses, cloth, linen, tweed, [and] flannel.[10]

Copy Plate. Infantry Approved by the War Department to Illustrate the Official Uniform and Dress of the Army, Issued June 6, 1861.

These lithographs printed in Virginia, were originally done in color. They covered all the branches of service, general staff, and included even the tailors' pattern for cutting out the uniforms. By the fall of 1861, finding a Confederate soldier dressed in the proper double-breasted tunic would be difficult. From Q.M. documents, this article of clothing was either too expensive or required too much work to produce in quantity—Jackets became the popular and requested article.

❖ Early War Period, 1861 – October 1862 ❖

He almost had it right!

This unidentified soldier has his frock coat piped in branch of service color, but lacks the collar and cuffs facings of the regulations of June 6, 1861. His frock coat is also single-breasted, a cut seen more often than the double-breasted version called for in the regulations. USAMHI

Confederate Lieutenant in Regulation Uniform

This young officer's uniform closely follows the regulations except for the length of the tunic, which falls below mid-thigh. If the volunteer soldier of the Provisional Army of the Confederacy found it almost impossible to acquire a regulation kit, his officers were expected to. Uniforms and accoutrements were to be paid for out of pocket and the regulations were to be followed. The cost, supply, and field use, would change all that in the coming years of the war. USAMHI

Russell also was unimpressed with the Tennessee troops garrisoning Randolph Point near Memphis in July 1861:

> Few of the soldiers were in any kind of uniform, and such uniforms as I saw were in very bad taste, and consisted of gaudy facings and stripes on very strange garments. They were armed with old pattern percussion muskets and their ammunition pouches were of diverse sorts. Shoes often bad, knapsacks scarce, head pieces of every kind and shape – badges worked on the front and side, tinsel in much respect. Every man had a tin water flask and blanket.[11]

In the camps around Lynchburg and Richmond, Virginia, the troops did not show up much better:

> From Lynchburg, Virginia
> Late Fall, 1861
>
> The [spectacle] which a regiment presents on parade is remarkable to the eye of the European. Many are composed of companies who have uniforms of different colors; but in these cases is always some distinctive badge by which their Corp can be easily told. This defect...is being quickly remedied, as we saw numerous regiments which had arrived lately, whose dress was all that the Horse Guards could desire.[12]

Another observer touring the camps expected to find, "half-clad regiments, instead of which we failed during our many rides...to see not one man unclad in serviceable attire. It is excepted that winter clothing would be served out before the 1st of November, and that the dress would become more uniform."[13]

Unknown Virginia Confederate Infantryman. Ready for war!

An early volunteer fully equipped for the upcoming campaigns of 1861-62. His uniform, accoutrements, and cap are all of Southern manufacture. How much and what was issued to a Confederate soldier was dependent on several factors, over which he had no control.

Private William P. Bond, Co. A, 6th Tennessee Infantry, 1861.

"Uniforms...in very bad taste, and tinsel in much respect...."

Private Bond in this portrait shows off his tinsel! His uniform does not conform to any known regulations. Tinsel refers to all the hat decoration, brass stars, ribbons, and feathers, all to add that bit of dash to a homemade uniform.

Brigadier General Sterling M. Price, to entice his rag-tag Missouri State Guard to join the Confederate Army promised, "The volunteer corps will be armed, equipped, tented, and clothed by the Government, with as much uniformity as possible, out of supplies they shall receive."[14]

A private in the 3rd Tennessee Infantry, Enoch Hancock, while encamped near Bowling Green, Kentucky, in November 1861 wrote home: "I have drawn one of the heavy Army overcoats and will have no use for the other one, [sent from home]. Captain Clark made a requisition, and wants the whole company uniformed alike."[15]

Shortages of gray cloth, a naval blockade, speculation, poor communication with Richmond, untrained officers, fortunes of war, etc., etc., were the real reasons for what one eyewitness described as the, "usual absence of uniformity," seen among Confederate troops.

The arrival of cooler weather that fall of 1861, coupled with a summer of hard campaigning, would contribute even more to the mix in Confederate clothing.

PART THREE

"Never has there been a more patriotic people than ours!"

J. B. Jones, Richmond.

The first and second Great Appeals of the Confederate States Government have never been given their proper place in the study and history of C. S. clothing. The Appeals are often overlooked as simply the work of a few determined Ladies Military Sewing Clubs, knitting socks for the boys at the front. Officially government sponsored, and with full support of the Quartermaster Department, the Appeals would contribute and be the primary source of clothing for all the armies in the Confederacy during the first winter of the war, and well into the next.

By August 1861, the Confederate Quartermaster General reported his Department woefully short of enough warm woolen clothing needed by the armies that winter. The Secretary of War was informed of the situation and told little else could be done. The only suggestion given was to try and get the needed supplies from overseas, but a second suggestion was sent by the State of Tennessee.

The idea for an Appeal came originally in correspondence to Richmond by a committee made up of some interested and concerned citizens of Fayetteville, Tennessee. The letter dated July 29 asked the simple question, "Can the [Q.M.] Department furnish all our soldiers with socks, shoes, coats, blankets, and shirts, and every other article necessary to constitute a soldiers winter dress?" They wanted to know, "if Richmond was unable to provide for the soldiers...whether the Government wanted aid and cooperation in the [matter].[1]

The Committee suggested that, "if the Government has to rely on the private contribution, that some plan be adopted at Richmond by the Department, looking to the unity of the people of every County in the South...and said plan be published in the papers."[2]

Walker did adopt their plan, issuing an official letter to all Southern governors dated August 7, 1861. It read in part:

> You are requested to have made up at an early date, to the extent of your ability, any woolen clothing to supply the needs of the Army, to be charged to the Government. [You are] doubtless aware of the difficulty of procuring a full provision in consequence of the blockading of our ports, and the limited quantity of goods in the market place.[3]

The first governor to reply was John Letcher of Virginia, who wanted to know, "what part of cloth-

Leroy P. Walker (1811-1884).
First Secretary of War for the Confederate States.

An important political figure from Alabama and an ardent secessionist, Walker was nominated for the position of Secretary of War on February 21, 1861. Claiming ill health, Walker resigned his post on September 17, 1861. His real reasons for leaving were whispered rumors of his incompetence and his aloof attitude when dealing with other Southern leaders including President Jefferson Davis. Walker received the blame within the ranks, and in Richmond, for all the confusion in arming and equipping the army. Walker was concerned with the well-being of the common soldier, supporting and implementing the first Great Appeal for donated clothing on August 7, 1861.

ing do you desire me to have prepared, coats, overcoats, vests, or pantaloons, or full suits?"[4] Letcher was very concerned with his state's ability to contribute because the C.S. Government had taken over control of Virginia's textile mills and State Quartermaster operations. The Secretary of War responded by saying that Virginia did not have to take part in the Appeal under the circumstances. Virginia's citizens would not be left out, however, and her people began to collect and make clothing for the needy soldiers.

Governor Brown of Georgia asked Richmond, "it being now difficult to supply clothing in uniforms, will clothing be required in uniform or will any substantial clothing do?"[5] The new Acting Secretary of War, Judah P. Benjamin answered, "it is not required that clothing furnished by the States be in uniform in order to be excepted." Benjamin in the emergency wanted, "anything warm and well made that protects a soldier's health from the elements as acceptable."[6]

The response from the Southern people was overwhelming. A Mr. John B. Jones, who kept a diary all through the war while working in the Passport Office in Richmond, exclaimed:

> Never was there such a patriotic people as ours! Their blood and their wealth are laid upon the altar of their country...contributions of clothing, provisions, etc., are coming in large quantities, sometimes in the amount of $20,000 in a single day.[7]

The Appeal drive was effectively organized. Each Confederate state was to have appointed, at both the local and executive levels, chairmen or agents to help solicit and collect the donations. In the State of Texas, as an example, the following agents and cities were named as the central collection points or depots:

At Jefferson	W.P. Stanley.
At Henderson	J.H. Partson.
At Palestine	A.E. McClure.
At Dallas	Dr. Sam'l Pryor.
At Sherman	W.E. Sanders.
At Waco	J.W. Speight.
At Austin	W.H.D. Carrington.
At San Antonio	Vance & Brothers.
At Victoria	Wm. M. Glass.
At Houston	E.W. Taylor.
At Beaumont	John J. Herring.

It was their job to receive and forward to the proper destinations the contributions of the county associations, and of the citizens generally. Also, whenever necessary to furnish transportation, "out of the discharge of their duties."[8]

The outlying county societies in Texas were to forward their clothing articles to the most convenient or accessible depots. All the donated clothing was then to be forwarded to either Jefferson, Houston, or Beaumont, to be distributed, "under the directions of the President of the Confederate States." Clothing, blankets, and shoes, if for general distribution to the Armies, were to be paid for in Confederate bonds.[9]

The ladies in Houston, Texas, went to work making up the heavy garments needed by the boys. From May 15, 1861, to January 1862, they turned out the following sets of uniforms, each company in a different shade of gray cloth:

> 85 overcoats, suits and pants. Co A, 5th Texas Inf.
> 84 overcoats, suits and pants. Confederate Guards.
> 6 overcoats, suits and pants. Gentry Volunteers.
> 12 overcoats, suits and pants. Co. F., 1st Texas Art.
> 5 overcoats, suits and pants. Houston Artillery
> 20 overcoats, suits and pants. Hickory Cavalry
> 20 flannel shirts. Archer Grays, 7th Texas Inf.[10]

One soldier in the Bass Grays, 7th Texas Infantry, wrote home proudly:

> We are in need of need of absolutely nothing. I notice the Texas troops are better uniformed than any other State. I have seen the Tennessee and Mississippi troops, and also the Kentucky troops. Texas is in no way behind these people![11]

From the *Little Rock True Democrat*, it was said that the support of the people of Arkansas for the Appeal, "would almost exceed belief."[12]

By October 1861, some $250,000 worth of donated warm, heavy clothing had passed through the collection centers at Little Rock. "Every county in Arkansas had contributed something," was heralded in the papers.[13] Wagons loaded with clothing were reported seen on every road and at every train depot across the State of Arkansas.

Georgia's war governor, Joseph E. Brown, advertised that he wished to purchase, "20,000 pairs of good, plain serviceable shoes, and woolen cloth, including country jeans," enough to make 30,000 suits of clothing. He also wanted all the good blankets that could be found in the market, promising to both the people of Georgia, and her soldiers, "never shall we permit them to suffer."[14]

The proceeds of the Appeal were reported weekly. For the last two weeks of October 1861, in Georgia, "$26,000 worth of clothing had been received for the 2nd, 8th, and 16th Regiments." Some of the articles coming in, "were not sent through the State Association in Augusta, but directly to the regiments as donations"! Another, "$27,000 for the Mississippians, $23,000 for the Alabamians, and similar amounts for the other States," were arriving every day.[15]

Contributions in cash for individual regiments were also tallied by the Passport Office in Richmond, and given to the papers:

> A. Rouse and E.H. Butts, $600 for the 3rd. No. Carolina.
> G. Peters, $500 for the 1st Maryland.
> M. Burgin, $2,000 for the 6th & 12th No. Carolina.
> J. Bason, $2,800 for the 6th No. Carolina.
> H. H. French, $300 for the 18th Virginia.
> L. W. Galbrath, $5,261 for the 11th Mississippi.
> H. Lecket, $690 for the 18th & 38th Virginia.
> T. Warren, $2,000 to Louisiana Troops.
> J. Cook, $1,115 for the 7th So. Carolina.
> M. Presley, $8000 for the 2nd & 4th Georgia.
> J. Carter, $6000 for Mantague's Va. Battalion.

An unofficial total in February 1862 stated that "contributions cannot fall short of three millions of dollars."[16] To the Confederate Army of Potomac alone, North Carolina gave $325,541, Alabama $317,600, Mississippi $272,670, Georgia $241, 884, South Carolina $137,266, Texas $87,860, Louisiana $61,950, Virginia $48,070, Tennessee $17,000, Florida $2,350, and Arkansas $950.[17]

A Confederate soldier writing from Richmond had nothing but praise for his new government, and said that all his needs were heartily supplied:

> Our volunteers were promptly paid the very day their wages are due, and never did a Government feed the troops better. In the Quartermaster Department in this city, clothing for the winter campaign is abundantly supplied True much of it is the result of private contribution, but this speaks the more for the patriotism of our people.[18]

Of importance to the uniform enthusiasts is what type of clothing was asked for by the volunteers. Writing back to their hometown newspaper the Clarksville (Tennessee) Chronicle, they directed their entreaties to the ladies:

> as to what kind of garments, style, etc. are wanted for our boys in Virginia, brown jeans pants, lined linsey shirts, linsey drawers, yarn socks and blankets. The color gray for the coats or jackets, which ought to be single breasted, but if gray cannot be had, any kind of woolen goods will do.[19]

The following request from the Central Committee of Tennessee appeared in the Fayetteville Observer, and is important as it specifically asks for brown jeans uniforms for the Tennessee troops in C. S. service:

> Clothing for the Volunteers.
> NOTICE.
> By the authority of the War Department of the Confederate States, we are authorized to say to those wishing to contribute winter clothing for the volunteers, that Brown Jeans for coats and pants, and colored linsey for shirts and drawers, are the materials adopted, and woolen socks with cotton heels and toes will be preferred, but any woolen socks will be excepted. If any blankets can be furnished by any person they will be thankfully received of any kind and color.
> By Order of the Central Committee.
> August 22, 1861, T.G. Goodrich, CHM.

The brown jeans uniforms were collected and shipped both east and west to the needy soldiers. Two Fayetteville companies serving in the 1st and 8th Tennessee Infantry had printed the following circular in the local paper to be sure they were not forgotten:

> All persons who have subscribed clothing, jeans, linsey, blankets, etc., for the Fayetteville Guards, Captain Ramsey's company, are requested to send in the jeans, linsey, immediately, and those making clothing will have them here by Saturday the 28th.
> J.B. Wright.
> Committee [20]

Let the friends of the 8th Regiment know we need shoes, blankets, shirts, pants, drawers, socks, etc. The person sending the article can mark the name of the volunteer on the article, and also the Captain's name in whose Company he is in. Friends of the Cause, I have tried Richmond, Va. for supplies twice, with little success.

> L. W. Ogelsby,
> Quartermaster, 8th Tenn. Inf.
> October 8, 1861 [21]

A greater part of the clothing donated for all the armies under the Appeal was described as the "handiwork of the fair country woman." Walnut-dyed brown, black, or gray cloth, checked shirts, wool or cotton homespun jean of the "bush" variety was commonly seen in the ranks.[22]

The winter of 1861-62, and the contributions of the Great Appeal, would see the continued development of that Confederate un-uniform appear-

**Private William R. Harris,
Co. A, 3rd Regiment Arkansas Cavalry**

Private Harris wears a unique uniform, even for rural Arkansas. He is also well equipped with a dagger, pistol, canteen, and haversack. By the fall of 1861, Harris and his pards would be asking for warm clothing, shoes, and blankets under the Great Appeal.   USAMHI

**Sergeant Jesse W. Carmack,
Co. F, 8th Tennessee Infantry**

Jesse's Regimental Quartermaster, under the Great Appeal, wanted shoes, blankets, shirts, pants, drawers, and socks, stating, "I have tried Richmond for supplies twice with little success." Sergeant Carmack wrote in 1921, "Sometimes we was badly clothed and fed, and sometimes we did well." Under the Great Appeal of the winter of 1861-1862 the 8th Tennessee did very well.

Drawing by Tom Arliskas of badly deteriorated photo at USAMHI.

An appeal for the Georgia troops in the *Daily Enquirer*, Columbus, Georgia, September 10, 1861.

They are our fellow citizens, our neighbors, our friends. They are enduring all the toils and labors of a soldier's life, in defense of their wives, our children, and our common country. Winter will soon be upon us, and it will be impossible for them to get, especially in Virginia, with the money allowed them whom for that purpose by the Confederate Government, such supplies of clothing, shoes, and blankets, as are absolutely necessary in that severe climate to their health and comfort. Shall we permit them to suffer for the necessaries, while we have plenty at home? NEVER! To prevent this I propose at public expense to purchase for them such articles as are most essential. Some of our manufacturers are making a good article of plain woolen cloth, others are making leather and shoes, while our ladies who have acted so noble a part, are in different parts of the State, making quantities of woolen jeans cloth. The soldiers are needing all we can spare! I wish to purchase for them 30,000 pairs of good serviceable shoes; and woolen cloth, including country jeans, enough to make 30,000 suits of clothing; further with all the good blankets that can be found in the market.

I also request the Clerk of the Superior Court in each County to act as Agent for the purchase of woolen jeans from the ladies…

— Governor Brown of Georgia.

Governor Brown of Georgia under the Great Appeal thought it a better idea for his State to begin purchasing directly the needed materials for uniforms, shoes, and blankets for the Georgia troops. Alabama, North Carolina, and South Carolina as well, started their own state quartermaster departments.

A letter from the Quartermaster General of the Army of Mississippi
for help in gathering blankets for the use of the army under the Great Appeal.

(This letter went out to every county in Mississippi asking for donations of blankets for the Army)

Quartermaster's Department
Army of Mississippi
Jackson, Aug. 20th, 1861.

Messr's Reynolds, Stevens, Esq.
　Brandon, Miss.

Gentleman,
　Will you take the honor to act as the Agents of the Quartermaster Department in receiving such blankets as may be donated by the citizens of Rankin County for the use of the Army.- You will also be authorized to buy such blankets as are in the hands of those who are not willing to give, but to sell them to the State, payable in State Treasury Notes at a fair price. You will, if you consent to act in the capacity, to please announce as your appointment as Agent for the purpose in the columns of the BRANDON REPUBLICAN calling upon the people to come forward and contribute or sell their spare blankets for the use of the soldiers. You will be responsible and hold subject to the orders of this Department such blankets as may be furnished by the Citizens of the County or the purpose named.

　　　　　Yours Respectfully,
　　　　　Jo.st Garnett
　　　　　A. Q. M. Gen'rl.

Company G, Fayetteville Guards, 1st Tennessee Infantry

On May 30, 1861, a member of Co. G wrote to his hometown newspaper, the *Fayetteville Observer*, telling how his company, "received our uniforms today… it is of tweed jeans. The pants have a black stripe down the leg; roundabout {jacket} with bullet buttons. The uniforms were made by a tailor in Richmond." That was in May; by August the Fayetteville Guards were requesting, "brown jeans for uniforms, and Lindsey for shirts, immediately for the company!" The Richmond tailors and the Q.M. Department were out of cloth and clothing for uniforms. The city of Fayetteville would supply their hometown boys.

Herb Peck Collection

ance, part civilian, part military, we have come to recognize as their trademark. A mixture of brown and gray jeans clothes, multi-colored blankets, hats or caps, whatever could be made into uniforms was shipped out to the Confederate camps.

It is impossible to estimate in dollars or numbers how much clothing was actually distributed to the armies that first winter. The Great Appeal clothing drive, along with that contracted through the Quartermaster Department, "made the difference between actual want and minimum comfort for the soldiers."[23]

Besides the clothing donations from the Southern people, states like Louisiana, Georgia, Virginia, South Carolina, and North Carolina, opted for a plan where they would begin contracting for uniforms at the state level. The commutation money would go directly to the state if they provided a uniform.

The system on paper seemed agreeable to both parties, but slow pay out of Richmond, along with a Quartermaster Department that sought direct control of all textile mills, would bring on the political argument of "States' Rights!" in opposition to the government's "impressment policies!" The American Civil War would be a frustrating four years for the Quartermaster-General's office of the new Confederate States Provisional Army.

"Poor soldiers, how you are imposed upon"

— Miss Mary S. Hall, diary entry, August 1861.

While the new recruits of the Provisional Army of the Confederacy were to provide their own uniforms, soldiers of the Regular Army were to receive them from the Quartermaster Department.

The first issue of clothing was to be: one blue shirt, (made into a blouse), three undershirts, two pairs of overalls, two pairs of drawers, two pairs of stockings, one pair of bootees, one blanket, and one leather stock, for new recruits.[1]

Recruiting officers stationed in Charleston, South Carolina, Augusta, Georgia, and Mobile, Alabama, were to requisition the clothing from Montgomery, Alabama, as well as any funds they might need in setting up their recruiting stations.

Contracts were let, as some of these Regular Army uniforms were distributed to troops garrisoning the coastal forts abandoned by the Federal Government. One soldier of the Regulars wrote:

> Pensacola, Florida
> April 6, 1861
>
> Our company have at last received our uniforms. It consists of heavy brogans, sufficiency of underclothing, gray homespun pants, and a yarn blouse, made like a butchers gown, (many a brass button!), and a glazed cap, giving us a very unique appearance.
>
> 1st Alabama, Tennessee, and
> Mississippi Regiment[2]

As the newly created Quartermaster Department administered to the needs of the Regulars, the War Department, in particular Secretary of War Leroy P. Walker's office, was flooded with requests for military clothing. Governor Joseph E. Brown of Georgia wanted either new uniforms or money for the men who had been garrisoning the Georgia coast since February of that year, and who were now threadbare. In response, Walker extended his "profound sympathies," pleading, "without an organized quartermaster establishment, and under the commutation law, I have no discretionary power by which I can supply clothing."[3]

Walker was concerned over the increasing number of complaints of poorly shod and clothed regiments. He called a meeting with the Attorney General of the Confederacy, Judah P. Benjamin, to discuss the problem. Walker's idea was to see if the War Department could circumvent the Commutation Law without applying to Congress for revisions which could take weeks to pass. Using the amendment of May 21, 1861, to the March 6 Act: "whereas commutation money set at $42 dollars a year be given, in lieu of clothing...received by the Confederate States", Walker ordered the Quartermaster to help provide clothing for the Army at large.[4]

It was Walker's belief, "that it would be impossible for the troops to furnish it themselves, and that it would be inhuman to permit the question."[5]

Colonel A.C. Meyers, Acting Quartermaster-General, ordered 5,865 gray jackets and pants out of New Orleans. Myers stated that if gray colored uniforms were not available, "any other color you can get, [send] to Virginia at once." Myers informed his special agent in New Orleans, J. M. Gault, to discontinue contracting for

The Approved Dress of the Recruits of the Army of the Confederate States. April 19, 1861.

In this letter dated April 19, 1861, A. Q. M. General Myers asks for one thousand Confederate States Army recruits uniforms. By June 5, less than six weeks later, the contracts were cancelled and the excess clothing was to be shipped to Richmond. All recruits for the Regular Army were to be sent to Baton Rouge under General Twiggs for reorganization.

Captain J. M. Gault
   Acting Quartermaster C.S.A.
   New Orleans, La.

Confederate States of America
Quartermaster Generals' Dept
Montgomery, Alabama.
April 19, 1861.

Sir;

The Secretary of War, having approved a dress for the recruits of the Confederate States Army consisting of the following articles, viz.,

Blue Shirt of flannel in place of Jacket to be worn as a Blouse as now issued to U.S. troops — double-breasted if possible — waist belt to be worn outside.

Overalls or trousers	Thin woolen — Steel Gray color
Undershirt	Flannel — Red or White
Drawers	Cotton
Bootees	
Stockings	Woolen
Blankets	
Leather Stock	Low "V" of pliable leather

Allowance per man six months, or until a permanent uniform is adopted.

- One upper Shirt or Blouse in place of Jacket
- Four pairs of overalls
- Three undershirts
- Four pairs of Drawers
- Three pairs of Stockings
- Four pairs of Bootees
- One Blanket
- One Leather Stock

You will purchase one thousand of each of the articles above specified for issue at once to Recruits at Baton Rouge, and New Orleans barracks, and furnish the clothing prescribed on requisition from the several recruiting Officers as you may receive them.

Make a contract for the delivery in New Orleans, in addition to the one thousand and each of the articles above enumerated.

Very Respectfully
(signed) A.C. Myers
Acting Quartermaster General

NARA. Roll 900-1, Letter Book. P. 104-40

---

the Regular Army, and to "purchase anything, jackets, pants, shoes, drawers, shirts, flannel socks, or have them made up as rapidly as possible."[6] Myers wanted 1,500 complete uniforms a week out of New Orleans, and directed the textile mills in Richmond, Virginia, and Columbus, Georgia, to increase their output of cloth.[7]

By August 1861, estimating the needs of the Armies, Quartermaster Myers reported that there were not enough shoes, cloth, or manufacturing capacity in the South to make up the 1,000,000 pairs of shoes, 800,000 yards of gray wool materials, and 500,000 flannel shirts needed for one year of service.[8]

In a private letter to the Secretary of War, Myers explained the impossibility of his Department to fill all the requisitions and asked him to use his influence to get the needed articles from overseas. Walker began a correspondence with several influential citizens on the logistics, financing, and the international politics of shipping in war material. Unfortunately, the wool clothing and blankets needed by the armies would not arrive for months, forcing Walker to issue the Great Appeal to the Southern people.

All sources of clothing, both civilian and military, were tapped that first winter of the war. The spring campaigns would open with a Confederate Army that would be multi-uniformed, but warmly clothed. A description of Confederate soldiers encamped near Norfolk, Virginia, in November 1861 reported:

> The uniforms of the different State troops agrees in no particular. As to equipments, the men are armed with the smoothbore musket, the only style of gun I have met with in the Rebel Army, with the exception of Bowie knives and shotguns.
> Regiments from Alabama, Mississippi, Arkansas, and one Texas Regiment, were all comfortably clothed, with overcoats and blankets.[9]

Some soldiers bought clothing on the open market or directly from the Quartermaster in Richmond. Private W. J. Tunnehill, Co. B, 4th Texas Infantry, in a letter to his father, told of the purchase by his entire company of "tolerably good overcoats with capes on them for $8.00 each."[10]

A soldier in the 10th Georgia Infantry was pleased to finally get his new uniform from Richmond, but was unhappy when the price charged for it was deducted from his pay and clothing allowance. "For a short jacket of coarse frieze, Virginia I think they call it, and a pair of inferior pants, they charge us $31.00! Great complaints are made at the General and Division headquarters on account of the miserable material the uniforms are made of."[11]

A subject that has never been discussed in detail, but which had a direct effect on the Confederate Government's ability to properly clothe their soldiers was speculation in the Southern marketplace. The $31.00 charged this Georgian was the result of artificial price hikes on items like clothing and food.

Speculation, the hoarding of military or civilian necessities, then demanding higher prices, had become a scandal to both the Government and the loyal patriots of the Confederate States by the fall of 1861. The Southern papers referred to these speculators as "wicked", army worms, and extortionists!" One fire-eating secessionist editor found them "even more disgusting than the Yankees!"

The *Memphis Appeal* reported that the price of clothing "had risen beyond all reason and decency." A Virginia gray cloth, which had been furnished by the mills at .70 a yard, was now being sold to the Army by the dealers for $3.50 in Richmond.[12] It was reported by the papers that a good cloth shipped in from Nashville for $2.10 a yard was sold again to a second party, and then sold back to the army for $10.00 a yard![13] At these prices, $31.00 for a uniform was a bargain. Acting Quartermaster-

Private James E. Wison,
Co. I, 10th Alabama Infantry.

Private Wilson's nondescript clothing is typical of the early volunteers who rushed to enlist in their country's defense. Armed with a shotgun and fighting knife, Wilson is the essential, "Johnny Reb" of 1861. USAMHI

**Private James N. McEachern,
Co. I, 10th Georgia Infantry.**

Private McEachern of the Fayette Rifle Grays, is dressed in what appears to be a Federal style mounted infantry shell jacket. The colors would be dark blue piped in rifle green. By the late summer of 1861, McEachern might have had to pay the $31 for a Government issue uniform like his mates in the 10th Georgia. USAMHI

General Myers made the statement in October 1861 "that in the last forty days the price of materials for clothing had advanced 100 per cent."[14]

Alabama Governor A. B. Moore, in a special report to his state congress, condemned the "extorting and extravagant prices [paid] for articles indispensable to the support of the Army" and ordered his agents "to purchase nothing from such persons." Moore added, "these attempts to speculate upon the Government and people are not confined to Alabama alone, every State of the Confederacy was infested with these men."[15]

The real victims of all this speculation were the common soldiers. Miss Mary Sophia Hill, whose brother was in the 6th Louisiana Infantry in Virginia, recorded in her diary that after only two months, her brother's company had already begun to "patch their uniforms."[16]

The threat of "Speculation and Greed" is editorialized in the *Memphis Daily Appeal*, of October 17, 1861.

Shameful Negligance.

The *Richmond Examiner* is positively informed that there are, at this date, detained en route at the various depots on the lines of the railroad not less than five hundred boxes of ready-made clothing, contributed to the army by the noble people of the South. The Government should take control of these railroads, at least so far as to require these goods to be sent forward. It is a matter of vital interest to speculators to detain and block the way to the timely arrival of volunteer contributions of clothing and stores for the soldiers, that it may not interfere with their greedy and criminal sales of cloth and blankets at four or five times their value.

**Private Reddick Walton Sibley,
Co. A, 6th Louisiana Infantry.**

Private Sibley's uniform by July of 1861 was threadbare. Some of his messmates began to sew bright red patches on their trouser seats to advertise their plight on parade. The needed new uniforms came a high price. One of those, *"imposed upon"* was R.W. Sibley. USAMHI

The much-heralded arrival of the paymaster on August 2, 1861, she remarked, created "much excitement around camp, as the men want new clothes." Her last diary entry for that day reported, "Sadly, those in charge (the sergeants and officers) began to speculate with the new purchases. A Sergeant Major J. brought in his own tailor, and Captain F. was selling tobacco. Poor soldiers, how you are imposed upon."[17]

It was evident to most Southerners that some of their neighbors were out to profit from the war. Greed was supplanting patriotism, and increased costs were being passed down to the volunteers. Many soldiers refused to take or buy clothing from the Government, preferring the cheaper articles sent from home. Those men who had no other choice were still paying for uniforms under the commutation law, long after the law was abolished in October 1862.

The Confederate government fought back by enacting legislation on price fixing and impressments. By 1863, they would control most of the textile mills and factories in the Confederacy. Inflation would be acceptable to the Southern people, but by October 1861, speculating would never again be tolerated. Those found guilty usually had their goods impressed, or if in the great state of Texas, would be drafted into the Army.

Operations of the Quartermaster Department through spring 1862 need more research. A report dated January 1862 shows that a list of all supplies and transport were being kept on account for every Quartermaster officer in the army. Returns and entries were logged, showing that the main depots (manufacturing and distribution centers) for clothing and camp equipage were in Richmond, New Orleans, Memphis, Charleston, Savannah, San Antonio, and Fort Smith, Arkansas.[18]

The same report commented that enough articles had been distributed, "and with the aid given by contributions of States and individuals (the Great Appeal) that the troops will not suffer this winter."[19] Prospects looked good for the future, but the number of wagons and the Southern railroads were found inadequate and inefficient for the present transportation of troops and supplies. The lack of enough transportation would have a direct influence on how the Confederate soldier would fight his war.

PART FIVE

"They looked like all the rest, a motley looking set of men in their various uniforms."

14th Mississippi Infantry
Fort Donelson, Tennessee
February 18, 1862

From the commencement of hostilities in April 1861, the Confederate military in the West planned as its defense to fortify and block the Mississippi River. Christened the "Great Natural Highway" of commercial and pioneer boat traffic, it was the obvious route for invasion North or South.

The Federal Forces moved first, occupying Cairo, Illinois, at the confluence of the Ohio and Mississippi on April 19, 1861. The Confederates countered by erecting fortifications near Memphis, Tennessee, and by seizing Columbus, Kentucky, on September 3, 1861. Columbus was a natural defensive position and was so heavily fortified and garrisoned that it was christened the "Gibraltar of the West," effectively blockading the Mississippi at that point.

On October 30, a correspondent for the *New York Herald* was able to sneak into Columbus for a glimpse of the Confederates. He was not impressed with the military appearance of the troops serving there under General Leonidas Polk, who had about 17,000 men, a mixed force of Tennessee, Arkansas, Louisiana, Mississippi, and Kentucky regiments:

> The troops were so rough, ill clad, and un-uniformed did they appear, that there seems a great room for improvement. About half the soldiers I saw there were uniformed, while the balance had an Army cap, coat, pants with a stripe or military mark of some kind, and the rest simply some ordinary [civilian] costume. Their arms were decidedly mixed...revolving weapons [Colt rifles], breech loading common muskets [Halls], and hunting rifles, etc.[1]

A second description from November 5, 1861 adds more detail:

> Shoes gave the most melancholy effect of the blockade. Those of leather showed numerous patches, and a long haired captain said a style made of cloth were being used instead. None of the uniforms on the soldiers were new. Blankets were scarce, and preparations for winter were scanty.[2]

I have already provided each man with his blankets, two flannel overshirts, two pairs of drawers, two pair of socks, one pair of pants, one overcoat, and one pair of good boots. What we cannot get here [at Columbus], is a suit well lined with cotton, made from the material manufactured in the Penitentiary, corresponding with that order by Mr. P.A. Ray of Point' Coupee, with brass buttons on the roundabout. This would be a comfortable, and at the same time, a genteel uniform.[4]

Battle of Belmont, November 7, 1861

As part of a major campaign to free Missouri of Confederate forces, the Battle of Belmont was fought on November 7, 1861. Belmont was located directly across the river from Columbus on the Missouri shore, where a camp of observation and a small garrison were located. In a see-saw battle, Union General U. S. Grant and a mixed force of some 3,000 infantry, artillery, and cavalry landed by steamboat and attacked the reinforced Belmont garrison, driving it from the field. Grant was forced to retreat when additional Confederate troops were ferried over and drove him back to his steamboats. Both sides claimed a victory. One of Grant's soldiers made a comment that the Confederates he fought against, "were poorly clad, but very well armed."[5]

A private in the 7th Iowa, in deference to his regiment's weapons (Model 42, .69 caliber smoothbore muskets) felt "their weapons superior to ours!" He added, "Every piece I saw was rifled, and there were a great many six-shooting rifles. Their Officer's uniforms were splendid and gorgeous, but the men's clothing were nearly all brownish-gray homespun."[6]

After the Belmont Battle, a special proclamation went out to the governors of Mississippi, Alabama, and Louisiana on November 21 for, "all the armed men that can be raised in their States as volunteer militia for sixty days, to resist an expected invasion of the Tennessee line."[7]

Three regiments of Mississippi State troops, appropriately numbered the 1st, 2nd, and 3rd Regiments, arrived in Columbus on or around December 25. Major General Polk pronounced them, "sick with measles, raw and undisciplined, and armed with every variety of weapons."[8] An article in the *Freeport Weekly Press* described the arrival of the Confederate reinforcements:

James M. Sarine,
Co. K, 2nd Tennessee Infantry.

The 2nd Tennessee received only a few blankets, shoes, and tents in November, December of 1861 from the Confederate Government. Overshirts were issued in January of 1862. A correspondent for the New York Herald said of the Southern soldiers he saw in Columbus, Kentucky, in October of 1861, *"about half"* were uniformed. The rest, *"in ordinary [civilian] costume."* Private Sarine is dressed in his everyday clothes, but appears ready for a fight.   USAMHI

Though it appeared the Confederates were suffering for proper clothing, a letter from an officer in the Point' Coupee Louisiana Battery dated October 28 stated: "up to this time we have been well fed, tended, and clothed."[3]

Under the commutation law, the volunteers still had to provide their own uniforms. Their Quartermaster officers could requisition or purchase clothing out of Memphis or Nashville if desired, but the soldiers preferred getting the articles from home.

Since the Battle of Belmont, Columbus has been largely reinforced. The Arkansas and Tennessee troops looked tolerably well clothed, but by no means uniformed. The new regiments from Louisiana [13th Infantry], and Mississippi [3rd Infantry] were nothing more than mobs. They had no equipments of any kind, and most of them wore blue blankets with holes cut out for their arms, and girded around their waists with rope.[9]

The 13th Louisiana was about to receive new clothing from the State when ordered to Columbus. It was mentioned that, "they will leave officers behind to bring it up."[10]

The Columbus bastion was considered to be heavily fortified for a direct attack by the Union high command, as was Bowling Green, Kentucky. They concurred instead to break the Confederate line at the center and attack Fort Henry on the Tennessee River.

Battles of Forts Henry and Donelson, February 6 - 16, 1862.

On February 6, 1862, Fort Henry surrendered after a pitched battle with the Federal River Navy gunboat fleet. The Confederate garrison escaped to Fort Donelson, but left an abundance of clothing behind. Not uniforms, but "clothing of the bush pattern, butternut jeans, onansburg overcoats, comforters, quilts, etc."[11]

Fort Donelson, located some seven miles away across a connecting neck of land, came under attack and siege six days later. The Fort was surrendered on February 16, 1862. An estimated twelve to fifteen thousand Confederate officers and men were sent North to internment camps to await exchange.

What was heralded as the greatest single Union victory of the War was recorded in hundreds of letters, diaries, and newspapers. Besides the battle itself, the weapons, uniforms, and equipments of the Confederates were studied up close. These were described in great detail for the folks back on the farm, as well as a waiting public up north.

The Fort Donelson uniform notes constitute the most complete and detailed set of descriptions ever seen covering one particular battle of the Civil War. The physical appearance of the men tells a story of an imperfect Quartermaster system, but of tremendous patriotism. It was the people of the South who obviously sewed and collected most of the garments worn by the Fort Donelson garrison under the Great Appeal:

The uniforms of the prisoners are just no uniforms at all, lacking all the characteristics of infantry, cavalry, or artillery costume, it being wholly un-uniform in color, cut, fashion, and manufacture.

Some have coats of a butternut color cut in regular saque style, and others fashioned like those of our soldiers as jackets or frocks. Their pants are as diversified in color. Many have no overcoats at all, and supply their places with horse blankets, hearth rugs, coffee sacks, etc., etc. Their knapsacks consist of bags [carpet sacks] of all colors and sizes, comparing well with their coats and hats. The same remarks apply to their canteens and other accoutrements, no half dozen of which seem to be made at the same manufactory.[12]

Some were clothed warmly, while others were very ragged, but such a thing as uniformity in dress was impossible to find, as there were no two dressed alike. Butternut colored breeches with a broad black stripe down the sides seemed to be the favorite running gear for the legs, while old blankets, patchwork quilts, a few coats, and considerable cheap cotton carpet made up the remainder of the wearing apparel. The carpet coats were made by putting a puckering string in the edge of a piece of carpet and gathering it around the neck. With the exception of Col Davidson of Mississippi, their officers could not be distinguished from the privates.[13]

There is no two of them a size, nor of the same dress, nor of the same color. Hats of every fashion worn for the last twenty years, pants of every hue of butternut brown. Coats of every fashion, as well as no fashion at all. Many had blankets over their shoulders, and they too of many colors. Some had pieces of carpet, others half worn horse covers, some had "old king cotton" shawls.[14]

The said uniforms of all shades of colors, gray, brindle, and butternut, the last predominating. Hats and caps of all shades, forms, and quality, and boots and shoes ditto. Even the six Rebel surgeons . . . are not better dressed, though some of them have made an attempt of distinction by shoulder straps and gold on their sleeves.[15]

In the way of clothing...it was evident no attempt was paid to uniformity. Coats, pants, and vests, were found of every known material, walnut bark dyed jeans greatly predominated. Most of the pants were ornamented by a broad black stripe down the outer seam,

Sketch titled, "Rebel soldiers disarmed at Fort Donelson—Stacking their guns." By Alexander Simplot.

This illustration depicts the general appearance of the Confederate soldiers who fought and were forced to surrender at the Battle and Siege of Fort Donelson, Tennessee, February 6-16, 1862. The contemporary description of, *"many had no overcoats at all, and supply their places with horse blankets, hearth rugs, coffee sacks, etc. etc."* is graphically shown here.

The Alexander Simplot sketch helped to uncover two mysteries of what was meant by, *"their knapsacks consist of bags of all colors, and…osnanburg coats."* The bags of many colors are everyday carpet sacks, and the osnanburg coat is shown worn by the fellow in the fur hat in the center of the drawing. Another recent discovery in the Watertown Democrat, (Wisconsin), added more details, *"The Rebel prisoners were drawn up in line, clad in butternut colored jeans, white cotton [osnanburg] overcoats, and all appeared rough and hard."*

The Palimpset. Vol. XLVI., January, 1965, No.1. Iowa State Historical Society.

Confederate prisoners captured at Fort Donelson, February 16, 1862.

This often-viewed sketch of the Fort Donelson Confederate garrison appeared in *Leslie's Illustrated Magazine* in 1862. Compare this picture to the Simplot sketch and note the similarities.

Privates James Jasper Adams, Thomas Jefferson Adams, and Joseph Joel Adams, Co. I, 14th Mississippi Infantry.

The 14th Mississippi Infantry lost 17 killed, 85 wounded, and 10 missing out of 650 during the Battle of Fort Donelson. The uniform of the Adams boys is probably wool gray jeans with red facings on the jacket fronts and cuffs. Facings colors on Mississippi uniforms changed three times in so many months. First, it was red, then green, then blue, by the Military Board of Mississippi in the early months of the war.

Emory Morgan Collection

Private John Dixon, Co. I, 56th Virginia Infantry, Fort Donelson, Tennessee.

Private Dixon's regiment was one of four from Virginia that came west to fight under General John B. Floyd. Private Dixon's trousers are marked with a broad black stripe, the unofficial mark of a Western Confederate soldier.

USAMHI

sometimes of velvet, but mostly of cloth or serge. Shirts and drawers are all of home manufacture, and of the coarsest description. I have a package of a half-dozen shirts made of a fabric many degrees coarser than canvas duck. Of these they had plenty. Hats and caps were diversified, yet they had a uniform cap – gray with a black band.[16]

Some of the Rebels had wrapped themselves in old patched bed quilts, which they had brought with them when they mustered into the Army. Others had covered themselves with white cotton blankets. Still others wore bright backing, evidently furnished by some merchant. One had wrapped himself in a faded piece of threadbare carpet. Their weapons were stacked, their accoutrements thrown aside, cartridge boxes, belts and ammunition trampled into the mud. The soldiers arms were a heterogeneous lot, single and double barreled shotguns, hunting rifles, flintlock muskets (some altered to percussion), and English manufactured Enfields.[17]

[On uniforms], brown predominated, but [some] were clad in gray – all shades, sheep, iron, blue and dirty gray. Most Confederates were in citizen clothes, their own military insignia being black stripes on their pants. Many officers had the regular gray uniform, while others the army blue, the only difference being a great profusion of gold lace.

For protection against the chilling wind, the soldiers used a conglomeration of overcoats, blankets, quilts, buffalo robes, and pieces of carpeting of all colors and figures. Each of the Rebels had a pack slung over his shoulder.[18]

Without any specific orders covering the uniform to be worn by the C.S. troops in Western Department No. 2, the black military stripe on the pants and the issue of a cap was an attempt to achieve some uniformity among the troops of the Army of Mississippi.

The brownish gray homespun jeans clothing, a gray cap, and brown jeans trousers with a black stripe were worn at Columbus, Kentucky, Fort Donelson, and later at Iuka and Second Corinth in October 1862. How long the sewing of black stripes on the trouser legs by the troops was carried on is an unknown. It might have stopped when a regular supply of clothing was available in uniform from the government, which should be mid to late 1863.

Battle of Mill Springs, Kentucky, January 18, 1862, and Island No. 10, Missouri, April 7, 1862.

Two other battles in the West were Mill Springs, Kentucky, and Island No. 10, Missouri, put under siege and its garrison captured in April of the same year. The uniform descriptions are not as detailed as Fort Donelson, but tell a similar story of brown homespun and an imperfect quartermaster system.

The troops who fought under Confederate Brigadier General Felix R. Zollicoffer at Mill Springs were, "well clothed in jeans, but they were without overcoats. Their discarded knapsacks contained two or three days rations. They were supplied with blankets of army regulation, white and black striped which were still baled when captured."[19]

At Island No. 10, near New Madrid, Missouri, on the Mississippi River, a protracted siege and naval bombardment caused the Confederates to abandon their positions, attempting to make their escape. Near Tiptonville, they were cut off, surrounded, and forced to surrender some five to seven thousand men. As to uniforms: "they had no uniforms, but were dressed as they left home, generally in homespun colored butternut jeans. Their blankets of every kind and color, quilts, table cloths, and carpeting were the material most were made."[20]

According to one Illinois soldier, only a single Confederate regiment was in uniform at Island No. 10, the 1st Alabama. They were wearing single breasted frocks of a dark blue jean material. These frocks were made for the 1st Alabama by the Ladies Aid Society as donations in answer to their appeal for new clothing.[21]

After Fort Donelson in February 1862, the Forts at Columbus were abandoned as well as those near Bowling Green, Kentucky. The Confederates retreated to Corinth, Mississippi, to consolidate and await reinforcements, and an opportunity to strike back at the Union invaders.

Battle of Shiloh, April 6-7, 1862

Their greatest single chance came at the Battle of Shiloh, Tennessee, fought on April 6 - 7, 1862. Unfortunately for uniform descriptions, the sources consulted give very little information on the appearance of the C.S. Army. If a description is given, it is usually color only, with little detail covering type of uniform or equipments. More work is needed on the operations of the Quartermaster Department just prior to Shiloh to get answers. The Confederates who fought at Shiloh were likely uniformed in a combination of both Appeal and Government Quartermaster issue, or State issue commutation clothing like those at Fort Donelson.

Private Leander Stillwell of the 61st Illinois Infantry remembered the men who overran his camp, Gladden's Alabama Brigade, as dressed in, "gray and brown clothes."[22] S.A.M. Wood's Brigade of Arkansas regiments were wearing, "butternut."[23] Some of Preston Pond's Louisiana regiments were still in dark blue. An artilleryman from Dresser's Battery was momentarily confused, as the enemy was wearing, "blue uniforms" and were carrying, "tri-colored flags."[24] After Shiloh, the Confederates retreated back to Corinth, Mississippi. A reporter for the *Richmond Daily Dispatch*, commented on the newly appropriated clothes the soldiers were wearing. "Unless we know better, a stranger could mistake our Army for first rate Yankees! Fully three-fourths of the men are dressed in Federal hats and overcoats."[25]

Private Histaspas Stewart, Co. C, 1st Alabama Infantry.

The 1st Alabama was captured, along with five to seven thousand other Confederates near Tiptonville, Missouri, in April 1862. Private Stewart enlisted in November 1861, and although dressed in gray frock coat and trousers, his regiment was said to be the only regiment captured at Island No.10 in uniform. The dark blue jean frocks were donated under the Great Appeal from Alabama. USAMHI

Unknown Private, Louisiana Crescent Regiment, Shiloh, April 6-7, 1862.

The silver crescent on this soldier's kepi marks him as a member of the Crescent Regiment of New Orleans, Louisiana. The picture is tinted. The trousers and jacket are steel gray piped in white cord. The kepi is medium blue and piped in white cord also. His rifle is a converted Halls of 1819. Many of Preston Pond's Louisiana regiments at the Battle of Shiloh were in blue uniforms causing, "momentary confusion" in the Federal ranks.

Courtesy Tom Molocea

The C.S. Soldiers had pillaged the captured Union camps, looking for trophies, clothing, weapons, food, and anything else they could carry with them: "We helped ourselves to whatever we could find. I took a fine carpet sack and filled it with trinkets, pants, cap, drawers, books, blankets, knives, India rubber knapsacks, haversacks, etc."[26]

A Lieutenant William R. Reid of Co. I, 15th Illinois Infantry, testified to the thoroughness of the Confederates. "We found our tents had been completely sacked. Everything had been stolen that a Secesh, or a [traveling] salesman could use. They stole my shoes that I had purchased in Waukegan, Illinois, and many smaller things."[27] Another Rebel soldier described his trophy from the Shiloh battle. "A large rubberized blanket

1st Brigade, 1st Division, Army of the West, June 19, 1862.

Ordered to reinforce Albert Sidney Johnston's Army in Mississippi, General Sterling M. Price and a mixed force of Missouri, Texas, and Arkansas regiments arrived in Corinth on April 11, 1862, five days after Shiloh. They were described while passing through Memphis, Tennessee, as "ragged and rough clad," and in "clothes of many colors as Joseph's garment." By September of 1862, little had changed. An inspection report stated, "Clothing; very indifferent generally, great deficiency in premium shoes, and necessary clothing." The loss of Memphis and Nashville as supply centers would take months to overcome by the Confederates, and Price's soldiers suffered for it.

From Headquarters
1st Brigade 1st Division
Army of the West.
June 19, 1862.

The clothing of the Command is wretched. Some are barefooted, many coatless; if a uniform in this season, not matter how light, cheap, or common were furnished, it would add greatly to soldierly bearing and their esteem.

Brig. General, Henry Little
Commanding 1st Division

NARA, RG 109. Price Papers.

Company B, 15th Tennessee receive clothing under the Commutation Law.

The 15th made camp in Tullahoma, Tennessee, after the hard marching and fighting of Bragg's Kentucky campaign, fall of 1862. While in Tullahoma, clothing was issued on November 21, 1862. Under the Commutation Law, a soldier was charged for each piece of clothing he took against his clothing allowance of $25 for every six months in service. The records show four different prices for the same item, "trousers." The trousers were likely made of four different styles or cloth, cotton jeans or wool, and maybe four different colors. "No two dressed alike," applied to the 15th Tennessee after this clothing issue.

18 blankets at $6.00 ea.	9 prs. of pants at $4.75 ea
6 blankets at $6.10 ea.	29 prs. of pants at $9.00 ea.
19 prs. of shoes at $4.50 ea.	34 prs. of pants at $9.50 ea.
17 prs. of shoes at $4.00 ea.	2 prs. of pants at $9.25 ea.
3 prs. of shoes at $5.25 ea.	50 jackets at $6.25 ea.
1 hat at $2.50 ea.	4 shirts at $1.20 ea.

NARA, RG 109, Regimental Records.

was my part of the spoils that came with the early surprise. In all my four years, I never saw a battlefield as rich in the legitimate spoils of war as Shiloh!"[28]

The Confederates abandoned Corinth on May 31, 1862. The Army retreated some 52 odd miles south to Tupelo, Mississippi to rest and refit. The summer of 1862 saw no major battles in the West until September, when Brigadier General Earl Van Dorn's newly created Army of the West began maneuvering toward Corinth, now occupied by the Union.

Battle of Iuka, Mississippi, September 19, 1862, and Corinth, Mississippi, October 3-4, 1862.

On September 19, 1862, the belligerents met near the town of Iuka, Mississippi, and a sharp little battle ensued. The Confederates under General Sterling Price, a mixed force of Missouri, Texas, Arkansas, and Mississippi regiments, were said to be uniformed in butternut, with the same black trouser stripes seen at Fort Donelson eight months earlier.[29]

On October 3 and 4, 1862, the Rebels came back in force to drive the Federals from Corinth. They were repulsed with heavy casualties, listing some 2,100 men captured. The southern prisoner's escort consisted of men from the 28th Illinois Infantry. One Union private referred to the Confederates as, "butternuts, miserable, shabby, dirty," and as to clothing, "all but naked."[30] As they were marched North as prisoners of war, they caused quite a sensation. "Nearly eight hundred Rebel prisoners passed by late in the afternoon. They were nearly all clad in butternut suits with a gray cap. Their knapsacks were made of rawhide with the hair on the outside."[31]

After General Van Dorn's attempt on Corinth, the tide of battle would shift farther south towards Vicksburg and Kentucky in the East. Along with a change in field operations would come a change in how the Confederate soldier kept himself clothed. The states, towns, and families of the South would continue to send in the clothing to those in need, but not in the quantities seen in the fall and winter of 1861. What the Columbus, Fort Donelson and Corinth uniform notes do tell us is at this stage of the war, August 1861 to October 1862, the Confederates out west were warmly clothed, generally in homespun jean cloth.

"The loss of public property has been great, and cannot be replaced."

Acting Quartermaster-General
A.C. Myers, October 10, 1861.

As Richmond concerned itself with operations in Virginia, in the Western Theater on the Mississippi River, the troops, though indifferently clothed and armed, were well supplied. Letters from Bowling Green and Columbus, Kentucky, Cumberland Gap, and the different river forts in Tennessee mention no shortages of winter clothing other than finding it in military uniform. Whole regiments were being outfitted at one time from stores collected in Memphis and Nashville, Tennessee, the main Q.M. depots in Department No. 2. The *Clarksville Chronicle*, in November 1861, reported that, "enough [Appeal] clothing had been received to supply the wants of Colonel Quarle's entire 42nd Tennessee Infantry."[1]

A military review held in Bowling Green a few weeks earlier had the troops dressed, "the majority in civilian type clothing, but a good many hundred of them were in uniform, and all were fully armed and equipped."[2]

All was quiet until February 1862, when the Federal Army and Navy attacked Fort Henry on the Tennessee River. Fort Henry started a string of defeats in the West that logistically and militarily would prove disastrous for the Confederacy and take a full two years to overcome.

When Fort Henry fell to the Union Navy on February 6, 1862, the Yankees were amazed at the stack of stores and clothing left behind by the Rebels in their retreat to Fort Donelson. One Illinois soldier described it as "enough to clothe a thousand men for a lifetime!' A mix of butternut jeans, onansburg overcoats, and bundles of comforters and quilts, etc., etc., littered the campground and Fort."[3]

"In the way of clothing, if the Southern Army suffer for it, I cannot imagine what would satisfy them", was the response given by one Private Miller of the 8th Illinois Infantry. "Every kind of baggage was left by them, clothing, uniforms, blankets, quilts, provision, . . . a vast amount of supplies captured."[4]

1st Lieutenant Albert Gallatin Harris, Co. A, 12th Tennessee Infantry.

Harris's uniform is of a pattern commonly seen amongst Tennessee officers in the early months of the Civil War. The two small stars on the collar signify the rank of 1st Lieutenant. The uniform is dark blue in color. Harris purchased this uniform in Memphis from the State Quartermaster Department. By February 1862, with the capture of Memphis and Nashville by the Federals, quartermaster operations would be moved east and south to Knoxville, Tennessee, Mississippi, and Georgia.   USAMHI

After Fort Henry, the Federals were quick to invest Fort Donelson on the Cumberland River. An estimated 12,000 prisoners, their arms and equipments, 14 heavy canon, and huge amounts of commissary stores were surrendered with the garrison. In a period of only two weeks the Confederate line in the West was completely broken. Bowling Green and Columbus, Kentucky, now flanked, were abandoned by the Confederate High Command.

One soldier who chose not to surrender at Fort Donelson was Lieutenant-Colonel Nathan Bedford Forrest. Forrest and some of his cavalry escaped, making a cold, slow, retreat to Nashville, Tennessee, arriving there on February 17. Another Donelson escapee, Brigadier-General John B. Floyd, had been placed in command of the post at Nashville. Nashville had been taken over by mob rule. Quartermaster warehouses were being broken into, and much of the C.S. clothing in storage as well as food stocks were being stolen or vandalized. General Floyd gave Forrest the job to restore law and order to a city in chaos.

Forrest did subdue the mob, but despite his efforts, over one-half of the Army's quartermaster and sustenance supplies were lost or abandoned. In his reply to a special investigating committee of the Confederate Congress, Forrest was unable to give the exact value of the clothing, shoes, harness, meat, flour, sugar, molasses, and coffee lost. He estimated it at "millions of dollars."[5]

Forrest, using the flat of his sword, was able to haul away, "700 large boxes of clothing, several hundred bales of onansburgs, and other military goods from the Quartermaster's Department. A large amount of fixed ammunition for light artillery, and 700 to 800 wagon loads of meat," were also saved, but he regretted, "most or all of the shoes had been stolen by the mob."[6] Forty pieces of artillery were burned or spiked by General Floyd's orders. All the rest of the war material would fall into Federal hands.

Forrest condemned the abandonment of these supplies a full eight days before the arrival of the enemy, and especially cursed Chief Quartermaster J. K. Stevenson. Stevenson had left on a special train (probably one he requisitioned himself), taking all of his "personal baggage, furniture, carriage, and even the carriage horses with him!" Forrest dubbed the entire affair the "Nashville Panic," deemed it entirely unnecessary, "and not at all justified by circumstances." He felt "that if the quartermaster and commissary had remained at their posts and worked diligently, the Government stores might all have been saved."[7]

Not all the quartermaster goods saved by General Forrest reached their destination. Much of it was hidden in barns or warehouses in Tennessee. A cache of army clothing was discovered by the 11th Illinois Cavalry in Middleton. Private Henry A. Allen found "boxes of clothing, mostly overcoats and homespun, white panama hats, homemade swords from old plowshares and scythes, and C.S. buckles and accoutrements," which the Suckers promptly burned.[8]

A Tennessee Pattern Frock Coat.

Research on the operations of the Tennessee State Quartermaster Department shows that the State of Tennessee manufactured and issued thousands of new uniforms out of Memphis and Nashville from May 1861 to February 1862. From photos, a distinctive pointed cuff with three buttons is seen on single-breasted frock coats. Regimental records and portraits of Tennessee soldiers show these frock coats issued through the state Quartermaster to the 2nd, 6th, 12th, 15th, 23rd, 31st, 45th, 55th Infantry and 3rd Memphis Battalion. The frock is also seen on soldiers from Alabama and Kentucky that passed through either Bowling Green or Columbus, Kentucky, in late 1861–early 1862. These uniforms were available for purchase to any troops serving in Department No. 2. In a letter to the Q. M. Department in Richmond, Colonel DeMarrin of the 2nd Confederate Regiment writes:

> All papers burned at Bowling Green upon evacuation. First transaction for clothing, $20,000 to Memphis, Tennessee, 600 uniform coats, 560 pairs of trousers for the 2nd Confederate and 10th Arkansas. 40 coats and 330 hats burned in the fire.

NARA, RG 109. Roll 1. p. 469. Letters received Q.M. Books 1-3.
See also *Journal of the Company of Military Historians*. Vol. XLVI. No. 2., Summer 1994,
Ross Brooks, "Clothing the Tennessee Volunteers, 1861."

**Private Robert Patterson,
Co. D, 12th Tennessee Infantry.**

Private Patterson is wearing a dark color Tennessee pattern frock coat in this photo, probably dark blue with light blue facings. In July 1861, the 12th was in Union City, Tennessee, with 737 men. They were armed with 1816 Model flintlock muskets. The regiment was transferred to Columbus, Kentucky, in September 1861. LOC

**Private W. A. Thomas,
31st Tennessee.**

Private Thomas and the 31st Tennessee Infantry were assigned to the garrison at Columbus, Kentucky on November 29, 1861. While in Columbus, Pvt. Thomas purchased his Tennessee frock coat, gray with blue or red facings. Courtesy-Thomas descendant by special permission.

A similar supply disaster befell the Confederates at Island No. 10 near New Madrid, Missouri. After a brief siege, the Union Army was able to trap the escaping garrison near Tiptonville, forcing a surrender. Over 3,000 rank and file, 5,000 small arms, 30 pieces of artillery, and what was described as, "a great quantity of blankets and clothing" were reported captured.[9] "The Rebels left provisions, clothing, and everything we need to make us comfortable," remarked a soldier in the 51st Illinois Infantry. In a letter home, the same soldier made note of the arms and supplies dropped by the Confederates in their retreat from New Madrid: "I have got me a Rebel coat, cap, and pants. They had hunting rifles, muskets of all kinds, flintlocks and cap locks. They all had knives made of old files."[10]

To reverse the fortunes of war for the Western Confederates, Brigadier General Sidney A. Johnston made an all-out attempt to defeat the Union Army with a surprise attack on their camp at Pittsburgh Landing. He was repulsed and lost his own life in the Battle of Shiloh. Again, the Confederates were ordered to retreat, leaving behind what one Yankee cavalryman described as "a continued line of destroyed army stores."

> It is impossible to give the description of the [number] of wagons stuck in the mud. Huge bags of flour in large heaps cut open so as to throw it out and get it wet, the same with piles of bacon. Stocks of poor clothing lay strewn around consisting of shirts, butternut colored pants, coats, and vests, etc., sufficient to furnish rags to the Rock River paper mill for a year. Tents and blankets lay along the road, torn, cut, burned, or trampled into the mud sufficient to furnish a large army.[11]

After Shiloh, the Confederates fortified themselves at Corinth, Mississippi. Under siege and outnumbered, they chose again to retreat, evacuating the city on May 31, 1862. A soldier in the 32nd Illinois Infantry surveyed the destruction done by the Johnny Rebs in their desire not to leave anything useful to the Union Army:

> We passed through the old Rebel camps, and in all my life I never saw such destruction of property. Hundreds of hog heads of mess beef and pork had been burst open and their contents thrown into wells or scattered over the ground so as to be entirely ruined. All cooking utensils, kettles, pots, plates, cups, etc., were rendered useless by the application of axes and hammers.[12]

By mid-summer 1862, the ability of the Confederates in the West to wage war was all but wrecked. The defeats suffered, plus the resulting loss of the important factory centers of Memphis and Nashville, were said to be the greatest single supply disasters of the Civil War suffered by the Confederacy.

The chiefs in Richmond were incensed, and called for a special investigation into the reported loss of millions of dollars worth of quartermaster and especially commissary stores in the Western Department. Explanations were also sought for the loss of Roanoke Island, and the hurried evacuation of Manassas Junction in Virginia.[13] In a reply to the Secretary of War, Acting Quartermaster Myers stated that he had asked for the reports, but none were sent to him. He finished by saying, "the loss of public property has been very great, . . .and cannot be replaced."[14]

For the Western troops now encamped near Tupelo, Mississippi, a period of want and suffering would follow. Letters and diaries give evidence that the shortage of warm clothing was particularly hard on them. One Confederate soldier of the 14th Arkansas Infantry complained, "our regiment is nearly gone to nothing. Our report to General Herbert this morning was 225 men in all, 82 without shirts, 96 without shoes, and 38 without hats. We are living on half rations, nearly naked, and no prospect for times to get better. The old 14th will soon go up the spout."[15]

In the same brigade, a soldier in the 12th Arkansas Infantry felt desertion might be a better choice than to suffer the cold and hunger. "There is defection in camp everyday. The men say they will all go home if they are not clothed and fed!"[16] Help finally arrived with a trainload of quartermaster stores, supplies, and clothing. The Galveston Weekly News reported its timely arrival, "as the [Army of the West] was much tested, one-third of the Army was without blankets."[17]

The First Missouri Brigade on December 24, 1862, was completely re-outfitted with a new uniform described only as "a gray striped blue."[18] Serving in the same Department of Mississippi and East Louisiana were the 26th Louisiana Infantry. That winter they too were issued new uniforms, "of Georgia woolens." Supposedly, they were cut to order, but as one private put it, "some fit, but a great many did not."[19]

Not all would or could be supplied by the Army Quartermaster. A general shortage of uniforms and shoes for late fall 1862 was the beginning of a period of discontent with the different bureaus in Richmond. A Captain J.J. Womack of the 16th Tennessee penned in his diary that, "our friends [at home] being regarded as a much more reliable source from whom we might draw from than the general government, it being at this time [October, 1862], rather poorly supplied."[20]

The newspapers were again full of letters by the different companies, regiments and battalions for donated clothing. From an advertisement for:

> McLaw's Division, A.N.V.,
> November 7, 1862:
> Quartermasters' Notice
>
> Persons desiring to send shoes, blankets, pants, jackets, or coats, drawers, shirts, socks, and hats, to the following regiments of McLaw's Division, can forward the same to the care of J.M. Newbury, Secretary of the Georgia Relief and Hospital Association, Augusta.
>
> The citizens of each county interested, are requested to send their contributions together, put up in as small a package as possible, (no package to exceed 100 pounds).
>
> Each article must be marked or addressed to the individual, the Company, or Battalion, or Regiment, for which the article is designed. For outside clothing, a gray color is preferred, pea jackets are preferable to coats. Only the above articles to be sent.
>
> 16th, 24th, 10th, 53rd, 50th, 51st, Phillip's Legion, Cobb's Legion, Georgia Regiments.[21]

A letter of thanks was addressed to the ladies of Augusta, Georgia, from the 1st Tennessee. Needy soldiers, even though cut off from home, could find succor from the many local aid societies in their area.

> Camp near Shelbyville, Tenn.
> January 20, 1863.
>
> My Dear Sir,
> I should not so long have delayed my acknowledgement of the kindness of the people of Augusta to the 1st Tennessee Regiment. Cut off from all home supplies, my noble boys found friends in Augusta, Roswell, Rome, and Savannah, who administered to their necessities. The following articles were contributed:
> 6 overcoats, 4 frock coats,
> 42 flannel shirts from Roswell,
> 304 shirts, 262 drawers, 200 socks from Augusta,
> 85 pairs of socks, 13 prs. of pants, 50 scarfs,
> and cash, $1,800, $600 spent on shoes.
>
> C.T. Quintrad,
> Chaplain, 1st Tennessee Regiment [22]

President Jefferson C. Davis pleaded with each state governor to assist the Quartermaster and Commissary Departments, "in procuring supplies of food and clothing for the army, and to put down the extortionists." Speculators were again driving up prices on commodities needed for the war effort.[23] Well clothed and fed or not, the Fall of 1862 would see two campaigns, one in Kentucky, and one in Maryland, in which both Army commanders would risk all to win a decisive victory before the arrival of winter.

Private Pleasant M. Wassom, Co. H, 16th Tennessee.

Private Wassom, armed with a Belgian conversion musket and single shot pistol, found little could be gotten out of Knoxville, Kentucky, or any other quartermaster depot in October 1862. Clothing sent from home was the only choice for many of the soldiers that winter of 1862-1863. USAMHI

Part Seven

"It is a sad parcel of soldiers here, who are now naked and barefoot."

C. S. Camp near Knoxville, Tenn.
October 24, 1862.

Leaving Generals Pemberton and Van Dorn to defend Mississippi, General Bragg began moving a small army to Chattanooga, Tennessee. His hope was to launch an invasion north into Kentucky in what has become known as the Perryville Campaign. But Bragg's army, in the words of one of his officers:

> ...when it started on the expedition, was not as fully equipped as it should have been. Many suits of clothing and pairs of shoes were wanted. Our Commanding General Bragg had many difficulties to contend with. He couldn't supply himself [locally] with everything [needed], and the different departments in Richmond gave him no assistance.[1]

An interesting and important find from the *Columbus Daily Enquirer* does show that Bragg drew some of his supplies from Columbus, Georgia. Columbus would become an important center of production for the Confederate Quartermaster Department:

> Some idea of the amount of clothing manufactured for the Confederate Army in this city can be derived from the fact that about 240 boxes, averaging three feet square and estimated to be 12 or 14 car loads have been packed here for a portion of Bragg's Army. All this clothing was made up in Columbus and its vicinity, and a large portion of the material was manufactured here.[2]

Only a portion of Bragg's army was supplied with these new uniforms. The rest received clothing from home or through state agencies. Uniform descriptions of Bragg's, "Army of Liberation," as he called it, are unfortunately few. The only account comes from the Official Report of General Patrick R. Cleburne: "As we ascended the hill, we were fired into by our own artillery in the rear.... I can only account for this blunder from the fact that most of our men had on blue Federal pants."[3] The blue kersey trousers Cleburne refers to were taken from captured Union supplies at Richmond, Kentucky, on September 17, 1862. Their old pants brought from Tennessee had already worn through.

After two-months of hard marching, the culmination came on October 8, 1862, at the Battle of Perryville, Kentucky. After a day of bloody fighting, Bragg's army was holding its own against a numerically superior foe. Bragg had wanted to join his forces with a second Confederate army under General Kirby Smith. Together, he felt they could defeat the Union army sent to confront them under General Buell. Bragg's plans were changed by Federal reinforcements, and the fear that his army would be destroyed if he lingered too long in Kentucky. Bragg ordered a retreat back to Tennessee, believing the Federal forces might gain his rear and block his escape route through the Cumberland Mountains.

Private Henry Elms,
Co. F, 6th Texas Infantry, November 1862?

Private Elms is shown here in a style of jacket referred to as the Columbus, Georgia, depot jacket. The rounded cuffs and collar of medium French blue are one of the distinguishing marks of this jacket. Both in November 1862 and April 1863, the 6th Texas was issued large quantities of clothing. At least one shipment came from Columbus, Georgia, if not both. Private Elms carries a Mississippi rifle, new canteen, cup, and knife. His hat is cold weather gear made of wool or fur. Diaries mention fur hats being sent out to the soldiers from home. USAMHI

Garments shipped out of Columbus, Georgia. Fall 1862.

A report from the *Columbus Daily Sun* of September 16, 1862, detailed the number of garments shipped out of Columbus, Georgia, to the Confederate armies. A description from General Tilgham's Division in November 1862, noted their "fine appearance…they had on gray caps and coats with sky blue pants. The coats are roundabouts—the cuffs and collars trimmed with blue," part of their new clothes from Columbus.

Jones and Farris. "The Civil War Diary of John Farris," *Franklin County Historical Society Review*. Vol. XXV. 1994, 53.

Supplies for the Army.

We have observed for several days large numbers of huge boxes being hooped and marked for shipment from the Quartermaster's department in our city. Upon making inquiries at headquarters, we find that within a short period of time, there have been made up and shipped from our city, supplies as follows;

Six car loads Clothing and Shoes for the Army at Richmond, Va.

30,000	garments to General Tilgham.
5,000	garments to Army of Western Va.
7,000	garments to Army of Arkansas.
3,000	garments to Texas Rangers.
17,000	garments to Bragg's Army.…

Courtesy Lee White notes

Major L. O. Bridewell and the Augusta Clothing Establishment.

An article from the *Columbus (Georgia) Daily Enquirer*, November 27, 1862, tells of how Major Bridewell of General Bragg's staff, was sent to Augusta, Georgia, with 23,000 yds. of Kentucky jeans to make uniforms. By July 1863, Bridewell reported he had 10,000 uniforms made up, but whether they were sent East or West is unknown. The Augusta Clothing Depot came under direct control of the quartermaster in Richmond in January 1863.

See also Les Jensen, "A Survey of Confederate Central Government Quartermaster Issue Jackets," *Journal of the Company of Military Historians*. Winter 1989. Vol. XLI. No. 4.

Clothing for the Army of the Mississippi.

We learn from a friend that the government clothing establishment at Augusta, recently removed to that city, has already manufactured some five thousand suits out of the jeans brought back by Gen. Bragg's Army form Kentucky. Major L. O. Bridewell of the Quartermaster Department superintends the establishment, and has been untiring in his efforts and personal attention to the work. Success has rewarded these efforts, and it is now hoped in a short time, that the establishment will be enabled to relieve in a great measure, the necessities of the Army of the Mississippi from the material captured from the enemy. —*Charleston Courier*

Sewers put to work for the Augusta Clothing Depot.

From the *Rome Tri-weekly Courier*, Rome, Georgia, December 18, 1862.

Work for the Needlewomen.

…During the few weeks the business has been in progress, a large amount of work has been in the way of making coats, pants, & etc. Hundreds of poor needlewomen have been furnished with garments to make up, and the highest price in cash is paid them for their labor… About $5,000 a week is paid out by the Government in this establishment.…The paydays are Tuesdays and Fridays.…A large corps of cutters is constantly employed in cutting out the garments. So far, we believe, coats and pants only have been given out; shirts and drawers will soon be added to the list…One dollars per pair is paid for pants, and one dollar and a half for coats. —*Augusta Chronicle*

On October 24, Bragg's army reached Knoxville, Tennessee, "hungry, clothing in rags, and the men's shoes completely worn out."[4] A Confederate lieutenant of the 28th Alabama Infantry, in a letter home to his wife, described the plight of his fellow soldiers:

> Camp near Knoxville
> October 24, 1862
>
> It is a sad parcel of soldiers here, who are now naked and barefooted. We have had a snow. The ground is covered about ten inches. The unkindest cut of all was that we had to throw away our knapsacks and all our clothes at Sparta, Tennessee on the 5th of September, and consequently we are now naked, barefooted, dirty, filthy, and lousy.[5]

Bragg, painfully aware of the condition of his army, ordered supplies of both food and quartermaster goods to be sent to Chattanooga and Knoxville for disbursement. Like Lee in Virginia, Bragg found out all too soon that the Quartermaster Department could not fill all the requisitions. Bragg instead ordered the Quartermaster officers of each regiment to return if possible to their respective hometowns to procure clothing by purchase or donation.

That same Lieutenant of the 28th Alabama was anxious to receive some new clothes from home. On October 31, 1862, he wrote again to his wife:

> Captain McFord starts here tomorrow after clothes for the Company, and this letter must address that subject. I want my overcoat, my boots, 2 pairs of drawers, 2 shirts, and as many socks as you have, 2 pairs of pants, a comforter, and a night cap. There was a small amount of clothing issued to the Regiment this morning. I got a pair of drawers, and 1 shirt of good stout domestic, and 1 pair of socks. I shall want a uniform suit. Get enough jeans from Mrs. Walters or someone else to make them. Lieutenant Mims will tell how to cut it.[6]

An artilleryman from Cheatham's Corp recorded in his diary on October 29, 1862: "Captain Stanford, W. B. May, Charles Roberts, and William Brooks detailed to go home after clothing. Some of the boys nearly naked. Hurrah for me — I was able to draw an overcoat this evening. Well boys, I am willing to divide it these cold nights when on duty."[7]

In an interesting sidelight to the Perryville campaign, it was reported that while passing through Lexington, Kentucky, Bragg took with him some 7,000 barrels of pork and $90,000 worth of jeans and linseys from Oldham Scott & Co. He planned to have the jeans and linseys made into uniforms. Bragg in his official report stated that it was enough to clothe his entire army. The *Atlanta Intelligencier* of February 20, 1863, had all the numbers:

> The following is said to be the precise statement of the spoils obtained by General Bragg and Kirby Smith's victories in Kentucky. Of the jeans, the total amount received was one-hundred and fifty thousand yards, which would make suits for ninety-five thousand men. Of this amount, Kirby Smith received ninety-thousand yards, and General Bragg twenty-three thousand yards. There was also brought out about fifty-thousand yards of flannel and calico.
>
> Of the captured property of General Kirby Smith's Army, there were six thousand pairs of shoes, three thousand blankets, two thousand overcoats, besides shirts, socks, and camp equipage worth $100,000.[8]

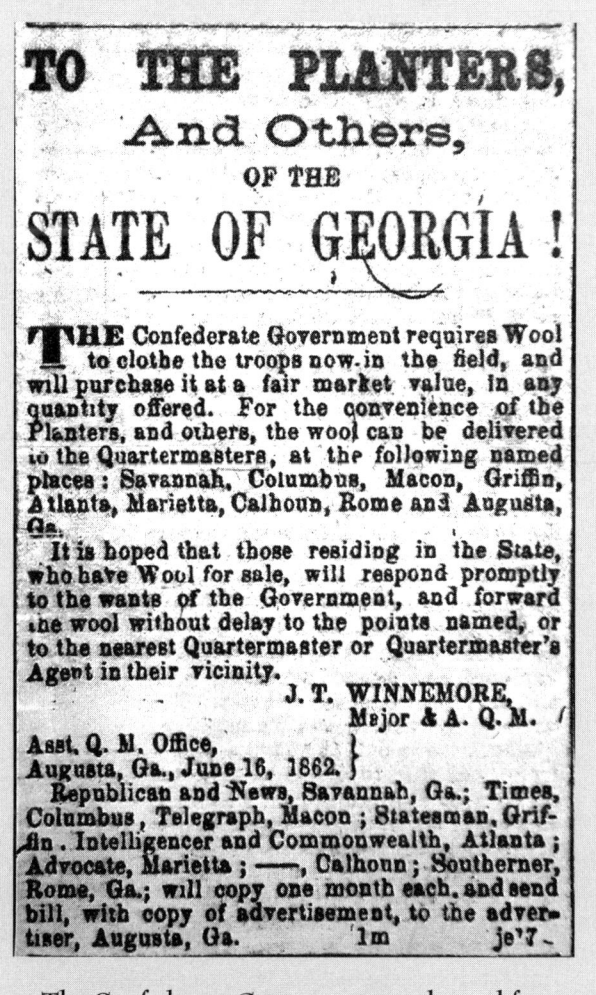

The Confederate Government needs wool for uniforms, *Augusta Chronicle*, July 23, 1862.

Bragg and his army took up winter camp in the Murfreesboro, Tennessee area. While Bragg's army recuperated from the Perryville Campaign, Union General Rosecrans moved out of Nashville to give battle.

Beginning on December 31, 1862, and on through January 2, 1863, the Battle of Stones River was fought. After a devastating surprise attack, the Union Army's right flank was driven from the field. Rosecrans was able to fight off the repeated attacks of the Confederates on December 31 and January 2, resulting in a stalemate on the battlefield. Bragg, against the objections of some of his officers, ordered a retreat south to Shelbyville, Tennessee. For the next six months, the Army of Tennessee enjoyed a period of rest and refitting, preparing itself for the spring campaign of 1863.[9]

"There were so many varieties of dress...they could scarcely be said to have a uniform."

Harpers Weekly,
Antietam, September 1862.

In Virginia, the Confederate forces were equally in need of good clothing for the opening campaigns of early 1862. As to a more uniform appearance seen among the troops of Joseph E. Johnston's command as opposed to the Army of Mississippi in the West, contemporary descriptions show the same mix in uniforms and clothing being used.

Peninsular Campaign April-May, 1862.

During the Peninsula campaign, the Yankee correspondents were very uncomplimentary when it came to describing for their readers those dirty and ill-equipped, "Rebel hordes." A special correspondent for the *Boston Journal* viewed the recently evacuated Confederate camps in the city of Yorktown and the large amount of food and camp equipage left behind:

> The equipments and clothing of the rebel dead were of the most miserable kind. No attempt at uniformity of dress could be seen. Here and there some officer had a flannel stripe sewn to his trousers.... The men were dressed in common linsey butternut and cotton suits of the commonest and coarsest materials. They had few knapsacks, being supplied with a schoolboy's satchel, sometimes of flimsy leather, but more commonly of cotton osnanburg, with here and there a rope to sling over their shoulders.[1]

The *Richmond Enquirer* of May 14, 1862, picked up from one of the New York newspapers their cover story on what was happening on the Peninsular front. The New Yorkers referred to the captured Rebel soldiers as being outfitted in a "peculiar uniform of a dirt-white color, covered with blood and filth. It is far from attractive. The long, lank, sallow faces, the black or flaxen hair, is all indicative of the Southern character, and proclaims them to be of such a type at the first glance."

Private William G. Howard,
Co. K, 35th Georgia Infantry.

Private Howard is armed and equipped with English military imports. Besides the black leather rifleman's accoutrements, he is armed with a two-band Enfield Sergeant's rifle with saber bayonet. His tunic and vest are of the same material, with black shoulder tabs. Although the State of Georgia produced thousands of new uniforms for its volunteers, Private Howard's dress could qualify as "*no attempt at uniformity.*" Howard was killed at the Battle of Frazier's Farm, June 27, 1862, during the Peninsular Campaign,

Leighton Young

These dirty, ill-equipped and lanky Southern characters turned on their pursuers at the Battle of Williamsburg on March 5, 1862. Rather than be trapped at Yorktown, Johnston ordered a retreat up the Peninsula, having to fight an unwanted rear guard action from some fortifications built outside the city of Williamsburg.

In a Confederate counterattack, several of them were captured, mostly men from Early's Brigade of Longstreet's Division. A Union sergeant, Fred C. Floyd of the 40th New York, made a comment that the rebels wore, "uniforms of varying colors."[2] Sergeant Floyd also, in talking with one of the captives from South Carolina, noticed that the buttons on his uniform had, besides the palmetto tree, the motto in Latin, "Anima opibusque parati." The translation means, "prepared in mind and resources," but when asked by the Union sergeant as to its meaning, the prisoner responded, "give the damn Yankees fits!"[3]

Following the siege of Yorktown were several battles in which Johnston and Robert E. Lee, his successor, countered McClellan's plans to capture Richmond. The first of these was a one-sided Union victory at the Battle of Hanover Court House, fought on May 27-28, 1862. The prisoners, mostly men of the 28th North Carolina from General Branch's North Carolina Brigade, were wearing:

> ...civilian clothes, but the mass adhered to homespun suits of gray or butternut, and the blue kersey common to slaves. Some were wrapped in blankets of rag carpets, and others wore shoes of rough, un-tanned hide. Others were without either shoes or jackets, and their heads were bound with red handkerchiefs. Some appeared in red shirts; some in stiff beaver hats; some in shreds and patches of cloth. In places I caught glimpses of red Zouave breeches and leggings; blue Federal caps, Federal buttons, or Federal blouses....
>
> In a corner lying morosely apart, were a Major, three Captains, three Lieutenants — young athletic fellows, dressed in rich gray cassimere [sic] trimmed in black, and wearing soft black hats adorned with black ostrich feathers. Their spurs were strapped upon elegantly fitting boots."[4]

Soldiers of A. P. Hill's Corps, at the Battle of Glendale or White Oak Swamp, one month later in June 1862, were dressed, "in a medley of garments, which would hardly be called a uniform, though gray and butternut were prevailing. Some of them had a strip of carpeting for a blanket, but the raggedness of their outfit was no discredit to soldiers who fought as bravely as they did."[5]

Union General McClellan was pushed back to the James River, seeking shelter under the guns of the heavy ironclad gunboats. But a new threat had developed north of Richmond. Another Union army under General John Pope was assembling near Manassas, about to embark on a second campaign to capture the Confederate capital. General Lee ordered General Stonewall Jackson to march around Pope's army to upset Federal plans for reinforcing Pope, as well as to disrupt their communications and rail supply routes.

One of the more notable Civil War exploits performed by General Jackson was the capture of Pope's supply depot at Manassas Junction on August 25, 1862. It was said over 100 box cars full of quartermaster and commissary supplies were captured, along with sutler goods of all types, like canned oysters, coffee, and cigars. "Twas a curious thing to see our ragged and famished men helping themselves to every imaginable article of luxury or necessity, whether of clothing, food, or what not," wrote one of Jackson's officers.[6] To further describe the situation:

> Fine whiskey and segars circulated freely, elegant lawn and linen handkerchiefs were applied to noses blown with the thumb and forefinger, and sumptuous underclothing was fitted over limbs sunburnt, sore and vermin splotched. Many a foot more worn and more worthy than those of the olden time pilgrims here received its grateful protection from the rocky soil" (translation: he put on a new pair of shoes.)[7]

A Confederate lieutenant recalled that, "the whole scene utterly beggars description. To see a starving man eating lobster salad and drinking Rhine wine, barefooted and in rags, was curious; the whole thing was incredible."[8]

Jackson ordered his men to take what they could carry and had the rest burned. All manner of Union clothing was donned by the Confederate soldiers. They would refer to it as "spoils of war." The use of captured Federal clothing would continue till the end in 1865.

Pope turned on Jackson at the Battle of Second Manassas, August 29-30, 1862. Pope was defeated by the Confederates and retreated back to the safety of Washington. By the late summer of 1862, after four months of hard campaigning, all accounts agree that Lee's army was reduced to ragged uniforms and worse, bare feet.

Antietam, September 1862

Descriptions of Lee's army at Antietam are many, and give an accurate description of how the Confederate soldiers of the Army of Northern Virginia appeared in the fall of 1862. A correspondent for Harpers Weekly commented on the appearance of the burly Confederates as they marched by, saying, "With the exception of their officers, there was little but homespun among them, light drab gray or butternut color, the gray predominating, although there were so many varieties of dress, half citizen, half military, that they could scarcely be said to have a uniform."[9]

Stonewall Jackson's Corps was in no better condition, his men wearing "dusty brown homespun, coarse slate colored garments, in fact all varieties of uniforms, and every shape, form, and apology for hats and shoes."[10] Historians agree that in terms of clothing, food, and especially footwear, the Army of Northern Virginia was destitute to the point of affecting its ability to wage war. Nothing was coming out of Richmond. The supply system on which the army's fighting capabilities were dependent, they believed, had failed them.

Diaries and letters tell of literally thousands of men who were forced to fall out of line of march due to sore and blistered feet. A Georgia soldier lamented, "I tried it barefoot, but my feet would not callous. They just kept bleeding."[11] One Virginia private joined hundreds of others on the side of the road, and described how, "My shoes had begun to give out, I had to fasten the soles to the uppers by making holes through each and tying them together with leather shoe strings. A device that did not prevent gravel and sand from freely entering the shoes to my great discomfort, impeding my march, and compelling me to fall behind the line."[12] And one of Jeb Stuart's staff, Major Heros von Borcke, was appalled at the sight of infantrymen, limping to the front. "I could not help expressing to General Stuart, as we passed the thin lines of our ragged weather-beaten soldiers, many of them without shoes, I did not think our Army equal to the impending contest."[13]

Another Antietam veteran actually felt embarrassment for the appearance of his comrades. Southern gentlemen having to suffer dirt, vermin, ragged uniforms, bare feet, and hunger was unimaginable a pitiful state of affairs for such a gallant army. "The lack of shoes was deplorable, and barefooted men with bleeding feet were no uncommon sight. Of clothing, our supply was so poor that it seemed the Marylanders held aloof from our shabby ranks. For rations, we were indebted mostly to the fields for roasting ears and the apple orchards."[14]

Although the 2nd Maryland Battalion did not fight at Antietam, a description of their uniform at Winchester, Virginia, by a Union prisoner shows them in sharp contrast to the rest of the Confederate Army. "The [2nd Maryland] were noticeable at that early stage of the War, as the only organization we saw that wore the Confederate gray. All other troops having assumed a sort of revised regulation uniform of homespun butternut, a significant witness to the efficacy of the blockade."[15]

After the battle, the grisly chore of burying the dead fell to the Federals. A Massachusetts soldier remembered:

> Many of the Rebel dead were lying about stiff and stark in their dirty white uniforms. Cartridge boxes, cartridges, broken bayonets, and knapsacks, cooking utensils, and clothing strewed the ground, much of latter having been taken from the merchants of Frederick City, and other towns through which the Confederates had passed.
>
> [We buried] Rebel boys of fifteen and sixteen, and gray headed old men. There was not to my knowledge in all that was buried any two dressed alike.[16]

A member of the 9th New York felt a deep remorse and sympathy for the enemy dead with their "poor pinched faces." All enmity died inside him. He felt that, "there was secession no longer in these rigid forms clad in butternut, just a pitiful waste in human life."[17] Word of the condition of the Confederate Army regarding clothing and shoes began to spread:

> I call upon you in behalf of my company. I might say all are without socks, ten or twelve are destitute of blankets, and until very recently, more than half of the company were without shoes. Socks, shirts, drawers, and blankets, I find difficult to get, the Government not being able to meet the demand. Besides, the high prices the men now have to pay for clothing render them entirely unable to clothe themselves comfortable with the amount ($50 per annum) which the Government allows for commutation.[18]

In a private letter to the *Columbus Daily Enquirer*, dated October 4, 1862, a Georgia soldier writes, "shoes are hard to get now, and they are badly needed too! I would gladly give $20 for a good pair of shoes, but they are not to be had at any price." One author, who used only his initials, P.W.A., begged for himself and his fellow comrades that, "we must have clothing and shoes this winter. Whatever must be done by the people should be done immediately! The Government is unable to furnish us supplies."[19]

The Army's needs were addressed by General Lee in letters to both President Davis and Secretary of War Randolph, who passed them on to Quartermaster Myers. Myers did not believe that Lee's men were so short of supplies and placed the blame on failure of the unit quartermasters to send in the proper requisitions. He condemned the waste of certain commanders who, he said, "requisitioned more than the troops needed." Myers also commented on reported cavalier treatment of Government property, that much of it was simply thrown away by the soldiers rather than collected and stored for future use. Myers was stung by what he felt was an unjust condemnation by both the Army and the Southern people of his department. He was so angry, when an improper requisition for shoes reached his office, he was heard to mutter, "let them suffer," a statement he later denied. Myers' position was, if Lee's men were cold and barefoot, it was the fault of their own quartermaster officers, not the Quartermaster Department in Richmond.

In Myers' defense, this tremendous waste of material was all too real, and goes back to the fall of 1861. A shortage of wagons to carry the men's extra clothing and blankets was the beginning of what was commonly referred to in the Confederate service as "marching light." From a soldier in the 2nd Georgia Infantry, dated November 5, 1861, comes this description:

> I do not like to find fault with our Generals, but keeping only baggage and clothing enough to keep oneself covered by day and night in this damp country is wrong. Let the men have all their blankets and tents, and if need be, let the

Two 19th Century "Pards" and two 20th Century "Pards" "half civilian and half military."

When a researcher comes across descriptions of Confederates like, "no uniforms at all," "a medley of garments," or "light drab and butternut mix," how do you convey this to the reader? What did the C.S. Army look like at Antietam, when according to eyewitnesses, no two were dressed alike?

These two pictures offer a candid view of what the Confederates might have been wearing for 1862. They show the old contemporary pards, one in uniform and the other in civilian clothes, and the modern pards taken at the 135th Gettysburg Reenactment. The resemblance is spooky between the two. The two modern figures' reproduction clothing show the drab gray or butternut jean frock and slate colored jacket, mixed accoutrements, and no shoes, mentioned seen at the Battle of Antietam.

USAMHI

❖ Early War Period, 1861 – October 1862 ❖

Government double the number of wagons for transportation, rather than have the soldiers suffering and dying from exposure and cold.

You take a musket on your shoulder, forty rounds of cartridges around your waist, and pack just as many blankets and clothing besides as you can carry, and you will find at night that you have not half covering to keep you from freezing. General Johnston may be, and is no doubt a great military chieftain, but in my humble opinion, he thinks, knows, and cares very little about the comforts of his soldiers.[20]

A second Georgia soldier of the 20th Regiment voiced a similar complaint. "We have only one wagon for every one hundred men, so you will perceive our wardrobes by necessity must be small."[21]

Upon the abandonment of the Confederate winter camp at Warrenton, Virginia, in March 1862, the destruction and waste of Army supplies was the direct result of a shortage of wagons and teams to haul it away:

Our tents and all our extra baggage have been burned, with a considerable amount of commissary and quartermaster stores, the transportation not sufficient to take them with us. Several hundred good blankets were burned by our regiment alone, and other regiments have destroyed an equal number, and all along the road you can see blankets and knapsacks that have been cast off by our poor foot sore soldiers.[22]

In a very interesting letter from a Mr. James Womak of the Georgia Relief and Hospital Association, he describes in detail the wasteful attitude of both the officers and men in the Army of Northern Virginia. He knew the work, sacrifice, and money expended to get the clothes and blankets to the boys, and was disgusted with the way these precious supplies were handled:

Staunton, Virginia
June 26, 1862.

I have been greatly delayed in my movement from the fact the Government has taken possession of the railroad trains, and are employed in carrying to Richmond the troops of General Stonewall Jackson.

Our Georgia boys are constantly coming in.... In two days time over 300 arrived mostly from the 13th, 21st, and 61st Georgia Regiments.

Knowing that a large amount of plunder had been obtained in the Valley, I asked why so many were without clothing, and was informed their baggage was in this city. A Lieutenant of the [12th] Regiment furnished me with 40 shirts, and 27 drawers out of the confused clothes, it being impossible to distinguish whose they were, no mark being on them. These are being washed, and will be distributed to the regiment. It was the best I could do, for very little can be bought in the city. Some inferior calico shirts were offered me for $30 per dozen. I thought it best to have the clothes washed and use them instead. On the long marches and in the charges of battle, our men threw away all clothing, and they ask for more! By a little oversight with the officers, much of this might be saved. I have just asked the quartermaster to have the blankets of the 12th Regiment dried and packed up. I had it all sorted in some measure. The trunks that were not broken, I had piled up and straightened.

The men go in with an order to go look for their clothes, take just what they want and pull over the rest. I found it painful to see the destruction of property. I found a box for the 12th Georgia in the depot, with 50 pairs of socks, 3 blankets, and 3 overshirts, etc.[23]

The simple task of saving or packing away extra clothing was not enforced by the army until mid-1863. The transporting of extra clothing or personal belongings, by the summer of 1862, became strictly forbidden. Stonewall Jackson, so as not to impede the speed at which his army could march, "ordered all the wagons containing tents and extra baggage to the rear, and as far as that, we never saw them again," pined one of Jackson's men. "This was a hard blow to us, since we had gotten into the habit of smuggling many articles into our tents to avoid carrying them, and when the tents left, they had dress coats, underclothing, etc. in them. Old Jack, flanked us that time!"[24]

To sum it all up, one old veteran felt that, "it did not pay to carry around clean clothes while waiting for the time to use them. The better way was to dress out and out, and wear that outfit until the enemies' knapsacks or the folks back home supplied a change."[25]

By the fall of 1862, "marching light" would become an accepted part of how the Confederate soldier fought his war. Carrying on his person only the barest essentials, he trusted to captured Yankee supplies, foraging, the folks back home, and the fledgling Quartermaster Department to keep him warm and fed. The old veteran, Carlton McCarthy, gave us a verbal picture of what those bare essentials were. "Reduced to the minimum, the private soldier consisted of one man, one hat, one jacket, one shirt, one pair of pants, one pair of

What started it all—"Sufferings of the Rebel Army."

The following contemporary newspaper articles tell the story of how the spectacle of Confederate soldiers marching through the streets of Petersburg and Richmond, Virginia, in rags and barefooted in the snow, would bring about the end of the Commutation Law. The Quartermaster Department was then made responsible for supplying all the clothing for the Confederate Armies.

Sufferings in the Rebel Army

A few days ago a scene was witnessed in our streets which at last aroused the people to a lively sense of the real conditions of our soldiers. A number of Regiments marched down Ninth Street, passing the very door of the War Department. Citizens standing near—there were no officials present; they never are on such occasions—saw with their own eyes what the papers have long and vainly tried to make them believe. They saw numbers of soldiers marching barefoot through the melting snow. Nor was this all. They saw them clad in ragged and worn out clothes; some of them without blankets and without hats. This was a spectacle to stir the pulses of a speculator!

But there were some who took good care not to witness so disgraceful a sight. At the very moment this barefooted procession was passing the War Department, the President of the Confederate States, his Secretary of War, all the Cabinet officers, the Quartermaster General, and some thousand of young clerks, were sitting by rousing fires, toasting their well shod feet and thinking of anything but the soldiers. It is not to be expected that stout young fellows, who slink into government drudges in order to get out of the army, should care about anyone but themselves....

Unworthy Officials.

As we have already noted, the people of Richmond, excited by the sight of barefooted soldiers marching through snow covered streets, have contributed some thousands of shoes to aid in relieving their sufferings. The President and the Cabinet, one member excepted, contributed liberally and warmly expressed their gratification that the people were thus aiding the government in the great duty of providing for the soldiers. Mr. Memminger, Secretary of the Treasury, refused to contribute, saying that the whole movement was a reflection on the government! He was willing, it would seem, to let the soldiers suffer rather than acknowledge the inability of the government to prevent suffering.

The letter from General Wise, published in our last, has received no contradiction or explanation from the Quartermaster General. On the contrary, Gen. Wise makes another publication in the ENQUIRER, making the statement more particular, and the Quartermaster's conduct more offensive. Will the President permit these unworthy officials to retain their positions.

Soldiers' Clothing.

The Richmond papers publish an important announcement from the Quartermaster General's Office, dated Richmond, Virginia, November 28, 1862. It gives notice that the Department will pay for shoes, blankets, and other articles of clothing which may be contributed by the people of the counties in the several States to their soldiers in the field, provided that such articles are supplied under the direction of the county authorities, — and offers the following prices for; caps $2, jackets $12, pants $9, flannel shirts $3, cotton shirts and striped cotton shirts $1.50, drawers $1, shoes $6, woolen socks $1, overcoats $25, blankets per pair $16.

The articles so furnished will be issued as far as needed, to the particular troops for whom they are intended—but if they are already supplied, will go to others. Payments will be made on delivery at the nearest Quartermaster's post.

drawers, one pair of shoes, and one pair of socks. His baggage was one blanket, one rubber blanket, and one haversack, his gun and accoutrements."[26] And all this because of no extra wagon space for clothing!

In spite of all the rhetoric on who was to blame for the Army's condition that winter, the much needed supplies began to arrive almost daily for Lee's men. From one Confederate soldier:

> Camp near Fredericksburg,
> December 8, 1862
>
> For some days we have been on the South bank of the Rappahannock waiting with great expectation the coming of the foe. Our Army remains in the best of spirits, and thanks to the good folks at home, our condition in the way of clothing etc., is daily improving.
>
> Large number of supplies for the 8th and 9th Georgia have been received in the last few days and more are expected.[27]

Another soldier himself encamped near Fredericksburg writes:

> I am glad to say to you that the efforts of Government and the Noble women of Georgia, have been entirely successful in clothing and shoeing our entire army. So far as I can see or hear in Virginia of a barefooted man, the clothing too looks comfortable, as well as our boys wearing them.[28]

A third letter to the *Charleston Courier*, dated January 23, 1863, tells how the spirit of the Army of Northern Virginia improved with good food and warm clothing:

> When I left these camps three months ago, the spectacle presented on every side was what might well have dispirited the most sanguine of heart. Thousands were in rags and destitute of the commonest necessities of life, and now as you move through the camps and see the soldiers in their winter quarters, observe the robust forms, bronze faces, blithe spirits, and thanks to the Noble women of the country, and the good citizens who have formed associations to help clothe us, that never since its organization has our army equaled its present fighting and physical conditions.

By the following spring of 1863, both army commanders, Lee and Bragg, reported their respective commands to in be good spirits, well equipped, and ready to campaign. The Quartermaster Department again had to rely heavily on the many patriotic relief associations to help meet the basic clothing needs of its armies.

Under censure for allowing the soldiers of the Confederacy to be reduced to marching barefoot in the snow in rags, the Quartermaster Department would have its entire system of operations changed. The year 1863 would find the Department ordered to provide all military clothing for its forces in the field. The commutation system would be dropped, and domestic sources would be supplanted by the creation of Quartermaster Depots, under exclusive Q. M. control.

As the year 1863 wore on, instead of C.S. soldiers being described as, "no two dressed alike," whole brigades and corps would be issued new military uniforms from one source or Depot. 1863 would be the Year of the Quartermaster.

**Private James W. Higgins,
Co. K, 16th Mississippi Infantry, Fall 1862.**

In this great photo of Higgins, he appears to have just come back from a summer of hard campaigning. The long hair and scruffy beard, soiled haversack, dented canteen, and what looks like a Yankee bummer's cap, add to the look of a veteran soldier. Higgins was wounded four times in as many minutes during the Battle of Antietam. One ball grazed his face and blackened his right eye and cheek. The right side of his face shows some marking. Higgins spent at least two weeks in the hospital in Boonsboro, Maryland, where he took the post of Commissary Clerk.

The frock coat with the huge pocket on the left breast looks new, maybe a gift from home or a pick up? The Quartermaster Department in Richmond took all the blame for the shortages in clothing and shoes for soldiers like Higgins. Many would rely again on the second Great Appeal of the winter of 1862-1863 for warm clothes, blankets, and shoes.   USAMHI

Confederate Prisoners from June, 1862.

This great drawing of Confederate soldiers captured in the field is dated June of 1862. These were part of Stonewall Jackson's Command sent by Jackson to draw off the Union forces under Major-General Fremont. A running fight on June 2, near Woodstock, Virginia resulted in the capture of 100 prisoners. The captions read 3rd VA. Cav. and Ashby's Cavalry. A description of Jackson's men at Port Republic has them in, "a {slight} apology for a uniform, others citizen's clothes with flat brass buttons, and others without even a brass button to designate their calling." These men look more like civilians than soldiers. Nothing denotes their being in service, than maybe the color gray in their clothing.

"I need the proper requisitions."

Condemned in the newspapers as uncaring and incompetent, Quartermaster Myers fought back. One of the reasons for a shortage of clothing was the submission of improper requisitions for clothing and supplies. Requisitions arrived in Richmond on pieces of scratch paper, unsigned, and illegible. The following original document for the 42nd Virginia Infantry for October of 1862, arrived in Richmond on a tiny bit of scrap paper. A second clothing requisition on file in the Wisconsin State Historical Society for General Morgans' Confederate Cavalry, although produced in duplicate, was not endorsed by any ranking Quartermaster Officer. Quartermaster General Myers was correct in demanding the properly signed paperwork be sent through his Office. That Confederate soldiers were suffering for want of clothing and shoes, due to paperwork, would change in the Spring of 1863.

✥ Early War Period, 1861 – October 1862 ✥

CHAPTER 2
Middle War Period, October 1862 – November 1864.

"The Quartermaster's Lament"

The Middle War Period was a time of transition. Private and state donations of military clothing under the commutation law, were to be replaced by the C. S. Quartermaster Department, as the main source for uniforms and shoes for all Confederate forces. On October 8, 1862, the Congress of the Quartermaster States repealed the commutation system as unreliable, and made the Secretary of War responsible for the collection and disbursement of all Quartermaster property.

Under General Order No. 100, dated December 8, 1862: "The Secretary of War shall provide in kind to the soldiers, respectively, the uniform clothing prescribed by the Regulations of the Army of the Confederate States."[1]

Under Article III, clothing in kind for three years would consist of,

	1st Yr.	2nd Yr.	3rd Yr.	
Caps, complete	2	1	1	$2.00 ea
Cover, cap	1	1	1	.38 ea
Jacket	2	1	1	12.00 ea
Trousers	3	2	2	9.00 ea
Shirts	3	3	3	3.00 ea
Drawers	3	2	2	3.00 ea
Shoes, pairs	4	4	4	6.00 ea
Socks	4	4	4	1.00 ea
Leather stocks	1	-	-	.25 ea
Greatcoat	1	-	-	25.00 ea
Stable frock (Cavalry)	1	-	-	2.00 ea
Fatigue overalls Engineers & Ord.	1	1	1	3.00 ea
Blanket	1	-	1	7.50 ea

For the first time by law, the proper military requisitions for clothing were to be signed and witnessed. Receipts, descriptive rolls, company books, and quarterly returns were required to be kept and turned in to the Quartermaster Department.

No longer could officers and soldiers pick over or discard unwanted clothing or quartermaster supplies. Each item of Government property now had to be accounted for, even if lost or destroyed in battle. Every circumstance was considered, the re-sale of deserters' clothing, issues to prisoners and convicts, the transfer and mustering out of soldiers, and the keeping of a list of damaged clothing and its value for resale to the ranks. The Quartermaster General was getting tough. One only has to read Article XIV. to understand how serious he was:

> In all cases of deficiency or damage of any article of clothing or garrison equipage, the officer accountable for the property is required to show, by one or more depositions setting forth the circumstances of the case, that the deficiency was by unavoidable accident or loss in service, without any fault on his part, and the damage did not result from neglect.[2]

Most likely, Quartermaster General Myers either wrote or had a tremendous influence in the writing of Article XIV. Quarterly returns were to be sent to Richmond. Clothing issues were set at twice a year, probably spring and fall, or in special cases as requested. General Order No. 100 was intended as an overhaul of how the armies received, paid for, and handled their quartermaster supplies. It did have one big problem attached to it. A clothing issue given only twice a year would not be sufficient enough to keep a man properly clothed in active service. According to one veteran of the Army of Northern Virginia, J.F.J. Caldwell of Co. B, 1st South Carolina Infantry, "most of the men rubbed out a jacket in two or three months, a pair of pantaloons in one!"

Caldwell's regiment, encamped near Moss Neck on the Rappahannock River in the early months of 1863, had just received some new clothing:

The North Carolina Jacket.

The Regulations for the Uniform and Dress and Equipments of the Volunteers and State Troops of North Carolina, 1861, state under Section 10: The uniform coat...shall be a sack coat of gray cloth...made loose, with falling collar...six coat buttons down the front...[with] a strip of cloth sewed on each shoulder...black for infantry, red for artillery, and yellow for cavalry. The State of North Carolina issued 27,380 of these sack coats, but ceased manufacturing this style in March 1862. Jackets were what the soldiers wanted. A shortened version of the sack coat, with a six or seven button front, and a smaller set of colored shoulder tabs were made. By summer and fall of 1862 a six button jacket was issued, without any facings, and with a stand-up collar. North Carolina produced many styles of jackets for her soldiers. More research work is needed on this state's quartermaster operations and the style of uniforms it issued it to troops.

Private Wesley Duckett, Co. C, 29th North Carolina Infantry.

Private Duckett is wearing the 1861 pattern N.C. sack coat. In March 1862, the sack coat was discontinued and a shorter version, a jacket, was produced instead. The State of North Carolina manufactured and purchased uniforms and supplies for its regiments until the end of the Civil War. USAMHI

Clothing was issued now according to the [new] system that dated from October 8, 1862. It will be remembered that before this, $50.00 a year in semi-annual payments was given the enlisted man in commutation of clothing. The value allowed now for clothing was $134.13 for the first year, $75.80 for the second, and $82.80 for the third. We could draw over this amount, and the excess deducted from our pay.

Few, very few, succeeded in getting into the debt of the Confederacy, except those who scorned to have their underclothing washed.[3]

Caldwell was also concerned with the effort and expense the Quartermaster Department put into making each Confederate uniform:

The quality was more to be complained about than the quantity. [The uniform] was coarse, stiff, and flimsy. Sometimes even cotton pants were offered us in winter. Scarcely a particle of flannel was to be had. The cut was worst of all. Anybody could put on the clothing, but scarcely any object in nature, except a flour barrel would fit it. Shoes were scarce, blankets curiosities, overcoats a positive phenomenon!"[4]

Taking Caldwell's observations as fact, a Confederate soldier would need a new uniform every three or four months instead of six, and the extra expense of drawing against one's pay to be well dressed was undesirable to most Confederates. It was better to trust your luck to the folks back home, the battlefield, or trading, than the Government.

Caldwell was not alone in his complaint of the quality of Government clothing. A Confederate soldier who called himself Cavalier supported Caldwell's testimony that the issue uniforms were not well made:

> Nearly all the clothing that we get from the Quartermaster is almost worthless because the sewing is sorrowfully done. Not a garment in ten will last a week without being made over. This is especially the case with shirts and drawers.
>
> If Government officials do not know when sewing is properly done, let our sweethearts have the material, for they know how to make two pieces of cloth stay together.[5]

The repeal of the commutation law was a practical move by Myers, for something had to be done by Richmond to keep the men better clothed. Politically, the Quartermaster Department and the entire War Cabinet could never again take the embarrassment and condemnation brought on by the field conditions suffered by the armies during the fall and winter of 1862-1863.

Quartermaster General Myers was adamant that if given the control he needed over resources, he could keep the armies well clothed. He would make the regimental and commanding officers more responsible for proper requisitioning and accountability over quartermaster supplies, and he would establish depots or government-run factories. Myers' goal was to eliminate the need for civilian appeals, which made his Department look inefficient and incompetent.

That the quartermaster system was beset with problems was common knowledge among the Southern people. Speculation, politics, departmental bickering, waste, and some very serious charges of corruption were topics of discussion in the Southern papers and around army campfires.

By the winter of 1862, a distrust, almost a disdain, for quartermaster personnel began to grow in the Southern ranks. They were referred to as "dandies" or "clerks in their gold laced caps and fancy white gloves."[6]

Stories like the following only brought more contempt: After the Second Battle of Winchester in June 1863, a member of the 49th Virginia Infantry walked into town hoping to, "get some of the spoils." He was told nothing could be issued to him except on General Ewell's orders. No matter how great the necessity, "[I] could not supply myself with anything."

While this soldier stood there and was refused any clothing or food, he watched as:

> every commissary Corp sergeant and employee in the Department drank lemonade and feasted. Those of the Quartermaster Department, sergeants, negroes, and all that belonged...were supplied with new suits, hats, shirts, fine gloves, socks, everything that fancy might call for. That was the reward brave soldiers received for taking the place, while "skulks" grabbed the spoils, this is however the case in almost every capture.[7]

Captain Thomas R. Meyers of the 41st Tennessee, in charge of the quartermaster stores at Port Hudson, Louisiana, upon the surrender of that place took the opportunity to supply himself with "some good clean shirts, socks, shoes, and a new and neat Confederate suit." These he took "out of a large lot of supplies we had and other supplies stopped in transit to the Western Armies by the approach of Bank's Army."[8]

Captain Meyers gave some new clothing to his servant, Abb, and to two of his friends. When he could, Meyers dispensed clothing to other needy C. S. soldiers while the armistice was on. From the viewpoint of the enlisted men, the conduct of these departmental personnel seems reprehensible, but they were following orders. Nothing could be issued without the properly signed requisition. Their flaunted personal use of captured and government

Unidentified North Carolina Soldier.

The young volunteer in this image is wearing one pattern of North Carolina jacket. North Carolina manufactured 49,345 jackets through September 30, 1862. The State issued 48,093 in the same period. Several different styles are evident in old photos. *Jeffrey N. Brown*

Abraham Charles Myers, 1811-1889.   Quartermaster General of the Confederacy.

Born in South Carolina to influential Jewish parents, Myers was groomed from childhood for a military career. He entered West Point on March 28, 1828, and finished 32nd in a class of 46 in 1833. In 1839 he attained the rank of captain in the Quartermaster Department. The rest of his military career would be spent with this branch of service. Myers was given the rank of brevet lieutenant colonel for his actions in the Battle of Churubusco during the Mexican War of 1846. His next assignment took him to Florida for the 2nd Seminole War of 1850. Myers was given the job of Chief Quartermaster for the Department of Florida. Assigned to old Fort Harvie, it was later renamed Fort Myers in his honor — a gift from his father-in-law, General David E. Twiggs, Department Commander.

On December 21, 1860, with his home state of South Carolina having left the Union, Myers tendered his resignation to the U.S. Army, ending a career of 32 years with the Quartermaster Department.

He was given the job of Acting Quartermaster General to the Confederacy on March 25, 1861, and given the rank of lieutenant colonel. He became the permanent quartermaster on February 14, 1862, rising to the rank of full colonel.

Myers worked hard in his new position using all he had learned previously. His responsibilities were enormous, considering his role of provider for 200,000 Confederate Officers and men.

Myers proved himself capable and was a powerful and popular figure in Richmond, socially and politically. In time, he fell out of favor with Jefferson Davis. Mrs. Myers was accused of referring to Mrs. Davis as looking like an Indian squaw. Myers was actually innocent, but was forced to resign after a lengthy political battle in the Confederate Congress on August 7, 1863.

The story of Abraham Myers is tied closely to the history of Confederate uniforms and clothing. Myers contribution to the Confederate war effort is almost forgotten, and he has never received the consideration due him.

Abraham Myers as Chief Quartermaster, Florida, 1850s.

Fort Myers Historical Society

Abraham Myers as Quartermaster General, Confederate Army, 1862.

Author's drawing from photo.

property would make anyone who was hungry, ragged, and barefoot, both jealous and angry.

Some were so angry that they blamed the loss of the entire war on the Department and Commissary Departments:

> Our Quartermaster Department really did a great deal more to break the army than keep it up. Their negligence, improvidence, and lack of energy, counterbalanced their services.
>
> Months on months [we] were without a change of underclothing, or a chance to wash that which we had worn for so long.
>
> As to purchasing clothes, the privates did not have an opportunity to do so once in six months, as their miserable pittance $12.00 per month was withheld for that length of time.[9]

Among the General Staffs, charges of favoritism shown by different bureaus in Richmond in supplying Lee's Army of Northern Virginia over other Departments were insinuated by the officers of the Army of Tennessee:

> The Government and chiefs in the various supply departments gave by far the greater part of their attention and means to the troops of Virginia. Their clothing was of far better quality [and] more frequently supplied.
>
> For our supplies we were more often dependent on our Commander [Bragg], who had to play the Quartermaster and Commissary General, and infrequently, supplies and clothing that had been collected [for the Army of Tennessee], by an order from Richmond, were transferred to Virginia![10]

The browbeating and corruption charges prompted one quartermaster officer to write a poem to his hometown paper in his department's defense, entitled,

Quartermasters' Lament.

> Horses and wagons and mules, barracks and quarters and tents.
> Axes and shovels and tools, haversacks, blankets and hats.
> Nails and iron and screws, pontoon bridges and flats.
> Fuel and kettles and planks, envelopes paper and inks, till the abstract I'm filling looks blank, and my brain is too dizzy to think.
> Will there never be an end to this everlasting issue, will the time ever come when the General won't miss you?
> I hope some day to go away, in solicitude to stay, where the horses draw no forage, and the officers draw no pay![11]

This same individual asked sarcastically:

> Am I a poor carcass of a Quartermaster, lean and lantern jawed, to be branded like an old worn out horse, with the letter "C" [Condemned]?
>
> It is a bad sign for a man to be pitching into a class of people and calling the whole of them thieves and swindlers, just because he has heard of a rascal or two among them.
>
> Here we work day and night in the mud and rain, and yet no word of approval, no vote of thanks, run almost to death with the responsibility of supplying beans and bacon, wagons and harness.
>
> The [Congress] have set the dogs on us. Well, it is very strange that all the rascals [who] managed to get into these Departments had somehow or other been sworn chosen or selected by somebody? Maybe the same Congress that now condemns us?[12]

With the commutation system abolished, those state bureaus which had collected the commutation money for their soldiers while they supplied the clothing, were asked to turn over the entire output of their mills and factories to government control.

Instead of a spirit of cooperation sought after by Richmond, states like North Carolina and Georgia were opposed, claiming negligence by the Quartermaster Department in keeping their regiments properly clothed. They felt their state's rights superceded any Government impressment actions, as to whom and where their products were to be sent.In fact, the reports of bare-footed and ragged soldiers in September-October, 1862, prompted the states of Georgia, North Carolina, and Alabama to place an embargo on all food, cloth, or wool and leather from leaving their states, and called out the militia to enforce their edicts.

On November 28, 1862, the state legislature of Georgia empowered Governor Brown to impound any cloth or leather from crossing State borders:

> His excellency the Governor of Georgia is hereby authorized to seize all the factories and tanneries and manufactured articles in the State, and to appropriate their whole production, till a good pair of shoes, and a good suit of clothes are furnished to every Georgia soldier.[13]

Confederate government installations, factories or their wares were exempted from this resolution, as were any persons who were acting under direct control of the C.S. Quartermaster Department in Richmond.

Governor Brown would not interfere with any contracts made before November 28, 1862, but anything remaining would go first to his needy Georgia soldiers, and at prices set by the Legislature or risk seizure.

The Governor of North Carolina, Zeb Vance, ignored the entreaties of Quartermaster Myers to begin turning over all the state clothing contracts to the general government. Myers notified Vance twice that the commutation contracts the department had held with North Carolina were no longer in effect, and warned him that no more commutation monies would be coming out of Richmond. Vance countered by saying that any change or renegotiations would have to be brought up with the state legislature. But apparently nothing happened as North Carolina continued to retain the whole output of its mills, a conglomerate of 40 factories and mills, almost half of the South's total textile manufacturing capacity.[14]

In retaliation for what Vance called an invasion of his state by "agents and speculators buying up North Carolina's military goods," he issued his own embargo on November 26, 1862, "forbidding all persons, for the space of thirty days from carrying beyond the limits of their State any salt, bacon, pork, beef, corn meal, flour, potatoes, shoes, leather, hides, cotton cloth, yarn, or wool cloth, without the proper paperwork."[15]

It should be noted that both Governors Brown and Vance were acting with the full support of their state legislatures, which were unsure that the Quartermaster Department could properly distribute clothing to the armies. Both states would enact programs whereby they would supply their own men without the aid of the Q.M. Department.

The abolishment of the commutation law, state embargoes, the Second Appeal, and public outrage over the ragged and barefooted armies seen in the fall of 1862 would have a direct effect on the field appearance of the mid-War Confederate soldier. For the spring of 1863, it would be again an army in mixed clothing.

"They were generally well dressed as far as comfort was concerned, but didn't present a very military appearance."

— Richard's Ford, June 1863.

Again largely provided for by donations, Lee's veterans presented a military, but un-uniform appearance:

> A group of some 200 prisoners, captured in the recent battles of the Rappahannock, [Fredericksburg] were the most miserable looking lot I ever saw. Like Jacob's coat of many colors, no two garments were alike being of every imaginable pattern and mostly of gray and brown mixture. Some were barefooted, while others were near to it, only two or three wore caps, the rest having on hats or handkerchiefs tied in turban shape to compare with their clothes.[1]

> They don't pretend to be either equipped or uniformed. All they want is a gun that will shoot, and carry their ammunition in their pockets instead of having cartridge boxes. Those who do have boxes wear them tied around their waist with a piece of rope.[2]

At the Battle of Chancellorsville in May 1863, a wounded Yankee soldier watched as the men of Ramseur's Brigade, consisting of the 2nd, 4th, 14th and 30th North Carolina Regiments:

> ...advanced to where [he and other] wounded men were lying. They made a soldierly appearance, though not a handsome appearance, as no two uniforms were exactly alike in style or color or material. The officers were much better dressed than the men; they had light gray uniforms, well fitted. They looked well armed and equipped, and as far as I could observe were under rigid discipline.

> Shortly, a Confederate Battery came up and lined up in our rear. It was the famous Washington Light Artillery of New Orleans. The officers were mounted and handsomely equipped; their men were more uniformly clothed than the other Confederate troops we saw.[3]

A Union soldier of the 146th New York Infantry made note of the appearance of a group of Confederate pickets near Richard's Ford in June 1863, one month later:

> They were clad in either butternut or gray clothes and were generally well dressed as far as comfort was concerned, but they didn't present a very military appearance.
>
> Some wore hats of black, some of gray, and some wore caps which we recognized as having been intended originally for use in the Union Army, but had been passed into the service of the Confederacy by right of conquest.[4]

Pender's Division, observed near Berryville, Virginia, in June 1863 had "serviceable clothing, as far as their boots, but there is the usual utter absence of uniformity as to color and shape of their garments and hats, gray of all shades, and brown clothing with felt hats predominate. The Confederate troops are now entirely armed with excellent rifles, mostly Enfields."[5]

Gettysburg, July 1863 — The Shoe Battle.

One of the more interesting anecdotes to come out of the Civil War is that the initial clash between the soldiers of Henry Heth's Division of Hill's Corps and Buford's Union Cavalry at Gettysburg, was the result of a search for shoes by the Confederates.

Lieutenant General Jubal A. Early reported that a shoe factory was located in the small Pennsylvania community. Early had occupied Gettysburg on June 26, with his division, spending the day in search of food, shoes, and hats. Under orders to march to York and cut the Northern Central Railroad, Early left town on the morning of June 27. He believed some supplies were still in Gettysburg, particularly footwear. Word was passed to A.P. Hill's Corps that he could find shoes and other necessities in Gettysburg along with some Yankee militia. What followed was the advance of Heth's Division to that place and the resulting battle.

When Lee's army crossed the Potomac River, they were in high spirits and well disciplined, but as to clothing and shoes, both were in short supply. One outspoken veteran, in reference to the efficiency of the Quartermaster Department, called the condition of the army, "most disgraceful, that fully ten thousand of men were barefooted, blanketless, and hatless, [when they entered Pennsylvania.]"[6]

This statement is supported by C. S. Lieutenant-General Jubal A. Early, who wrote just prior to the invasion that in his division of 7,226 men:

> ...about one-third of the men were without bayonets, and their deficiency existed in the Army owing in great measure to the fact that nearly all of our small arms had been taken from the enemy on the various battlefields.
>
> There was a great deficiency in shoes for the infantry, a large number of the men being indifferently shod, and some barefooted. A like deficiency existed in regard to the equipment of the men in other respects, the supply of clothing, blankets, etc., being very limited.[7]

The lack of good shoe leather on the hard surfaced Pennsylvania roads resulted in a disproportionate number of stragglers. One C.S. officer found it, "hard trying to keep the men on the move."[8] The ragged, barefooted Rebel was a common sight at Gettysburg in July 1863. "Many soldiers leave the ranks through necessity . . . others are barefoot, and many have thrown away their shoes, as an excuse for straggling, still their feet are bruised and bleeding."[9]

In May 1863, General Robert E. Lee, on the heels of his great victory at Chancellorsville, planned a second invasion north into Maryland and Pennsylvania. The plan was to first, take the pressure off Confederate General Pemberton at Vicksburg, Mississippi. Pemberton had been under siege since late May and needed succor, either in reinforcements or some attention getter in the East or West to draw off Union troops.

Second, and of greater importance to Lee's army, was to gather supplies up north. The Shenandoah Valley, Lee's bread basket, was depleted. The farmers had to have time that summer to grow and gather in their crops. Also, it was hoped the army could be re-outfitted by capture and confiscation from the enemy. Clothing, and especially shoes, by June 1863 had again grown scarce.

Third, Lee felt his men's morale was at an all-time high. He felt his army was invincible. One more great victory like Chancellorsville or Fredericksburg in the North could give the South everything it sought, recognition by the Europeans, and an even more war weary Northern populace.

As at Antietam in September 1862, descriptions of the Army of Northern Virginia during the Gettysburg Campaign are numerous. An Agent for the Union Sanitary Commission was able to sneak into one of Ewell's camps near York, Pennsylvania, and commented that the Rebels were,

"The color of a Reb is not unlike that of ripe wheat."

Major Robert L. Bodine, 26th Regiment Pennsylvania Volunteers, talks about Pickett's Charge to his hometown newspaper, the Doylestown Democrat, July 12, 1863.

I never before seen such desperation on the part of the Rebels, who hurled their columns upon us in masses, only to be cut to pieces… I was on the battlefield nearly all night on the 3rd, attending to the removal of my wounded… How the field looked by moonlight [like] a wheat field, where the sheaves have been left un-gathered, and the color of a Reb is not unlike that of ripe wheat.

The Brigade we were opposed were all armed with the Springfield rifles. Many of them had gone through the renovating process, and bore the Richmond C. S. stamp."

How were they uniformed?
Georgians at the Stone Wall, Gettysburg.

John Buckley of Co. K., 169th Pennsylvania Infantry, wrote to a friend how his regiment counterattacked and drove the Georgians back during Pickett's Charge at Gettysburg, July 3, 1863. "We took a great many prisoners, most of who were Georgians, and the best clothed soldiers we had ever come across on their side."

These were the infantrymen of Wright's Brigade, the 3rd, 22nd, 48th, and 2nd Georgia Battalion. Were Wright's Georgians dressed in donated clothing from their home state, or from the Richmond Quartermaster Depot? Either way Wright's Georgians made quite an impression of Private Buckley.

The Famous Photo of three Confederate prisoners at Gettysburg.

Although this photo has appeared many times in other works on the Civil War, it does tell the story of how generally the Confederate soldier appeared on the battlefield of Gettysburg, Pennsylvania, in July 1863. Dressed in gray or drab brown, in a short jacket, with a blanket roll over their shoulder, their equipment was light compared to the Federals. It appears that all have knapsacks, haversacks, and canteens, perhaps in preparation for prison camp.   LOC

...well stripped for action and capable of fast movement.

Physically the men looked about equal to the generality of our troops and there were fewer boys among them. Their dress was a wretched mixture of all cuts and colors. Their shoes as a general thing were poor, some of them entirely barefooted. Their equipments were light compared with those of our men. They consisted of a thin woolen blanket, coiled and hung from the shoulders in the form of a sash, a haversack swung from the opposite shoulder, and a cartridge box. The whole cannot weigh more than twelve or fourteen pounds.[10]

One Union private remembered that the Rebels he saw were dressed, "in gray and butternut and wore generally a short jacket, and a blanket strapped over his shoulder, and under his arm. A victory gave them Yankee boots, jack knives, and overcoats."[11]

Hood's Texas Brigade brought some special comment just prior to the battle. "They carry less than any other troops, many of them have only got an old piece of carpet or rug as baggage, many have discarded their shoes in the mud, all are ragged and dirty, but full of good humor and confidence in themselves and their General Hood."[12] And some of the soldiers in McLaw's Division were seen carrying captured Union knapsacks bearing the names, "Massachusetts, New Jersey, and other Union Regiments."[13]

After Pickett's charge on July 3, a Northern reporter wrote that the Confederate prisoners, "were poorly clothed in a variety of uniforms, a dingy gray color prevailing, some wore jackets, others gray skirted coats trimmed on collars and sleeves. Some wore boots, others shoes, and many were barefooted. There were many ragged slouch hats, and caps of various kinds with visors."[14]

The repulse of Pickett's charge on July 3, was the cause for Lee to issue an order of withdrawal for the army. Ammunition, particularly heavy ordnance for the artillery, was in short supply, as was food and forage. Lee had no other choice but to retreat back to Virginia. The Confederates, after a severe march and some heroic efforts to save their wagon trains from Meade's pursuing cavalry, made camp near Orange Court House and Fredericksburg, Virginia.

Again, as in the previous two winters of the War, hard campaigning and marching had reduced the army to rags and bare-feet. One member of the 21st Virginia Infantry described the Army of Northern Virginia as:

in a sad plight as to clothing. Hundreds had no shoes, thousands were as ragged as they could be.... Some of the men patched their clothing and it was usually done with any material they could get; one man having the seat of his pants patched bright red, his knees patched in black, another with a piece of gray or brown blanket, in fact with anything they could get.[15]

From these descriptions it would appear that the Confederate Army of Northern Virginia was just as unkempt and un-uniformed as ever, with little chance of improving their military appearance.

But improve it they did.

"Neat uniforms of gray jackets and trousers of light blue" [A.N.V.]

— *Bermuda Gazette*, September 1863.

The general consensus among C. S. uniform researchers is that starting in mid-1863, the Confederate armies, having to rely more on the Quartermaster Department, or better yet, the Quartermaster-General so ordered to supply uniforms to every soldier, began to appear on some battlefields all in the same uniform. The reason: a Quartermaster Department that through a thorough reorganization and a greater reliance on imports, was producing thousands of new uniforms every month in the different depots set up all over the South.

Under General Order No. 13 dated January 31, 1863, the several arsenals, armories, depots, etc., were to be put under immediate charge of the War Department, and its orders were to come directly out of the Ordnance Bureau in Richmond. Article IV stated that the Quartermaster Depots at Augusta, Atlanta, and Columbus, Georgia, and Montgomery and Huntsville, Alabama, were now to be placed under the special control of the Quartermaster-General in Richmond. Issues from these depots were to be filled only on order of the Quartermaster-General. All clothing requisitioned out of depot stocks were to be approved first by the commanding generals and their staffs. The generals assumed part of the responsibility for any waste or shortages among their soldiers.

A second circular dated March 24, 1863, came out of the Quartermaster-General's office, and was approved by the Secretary of War, naming eleven quartermaster officers to have exclusive control over eleven state districts and the quartermaster operations therein. This was done to avoid any conflict or competition between the officers of the Quartermaster Department and those of the Ordnance and Commissary Bureaus in purchasing of supplies common to both.[1]

Main depots (set up for the armies), were to be established at Richmond and Staunton, Virginia; Raleigh, North Carolina; Columbus and Atlanta, Georgia; Huntsville and Montgomery, Alabama; Jackson, Mississippi; Alexandria, Louisiana; Little Rock, Arkansas; Knoxville, Tennessee; San Antonio, Texas; or elsewhere, as hereafter indicated. All of these depots were now under the exclusive control of the Quartermaster-General's office. This was done in the spring

Special Notice.
Quartermaster Department. March 18, 1863.

A new rule that came with the overhaul of the Confederate Quartermaster Department in early 1863 was that quartermaster personnel working in Beauregard's Southern Department now had to report in.

Augusta (Georgia) Chronicle, April 21, 1863

"Never put your contributions in the hands of government agents of any sort." A warning from the *Rome (Georgia) Tri-weekly Courier.* November 1, 1862.

of 1863 to keep prices down, to regulate the number of purchasing agents operating in a particular district, and to place even more control over the limited resources of the South.

A report for the last two quarters of 1864 through January 1865 does exist, but nothing as detailed as before June 1864, to my knowledge, has been found. What is available on the operations of some of the different depots and state bureaus is as follows.

Augusta, Georgia

In Augusta, Georgia, to help Georgia soldiers during the winter of 1862-63, the state appropriated $1,500,000 to start a Georgia Soldiers Bureau of Augusta. It was reported to be turning out 500 garments a day, employing 500 women, each making from $6.00 to $12.00 a week.

> As fast as garments are completed, they are inspected and if accepted, marked Georgia Soldiers Clothing Bureau, Augusta, Georgia, and boxed for shipment. The Bureau is auxiliary to the facilities afforded by the Confederate Government and will, it is believed, alleviate any want to clothing that may, from any cause, exist among Georgia troops.

Its Director was pleased to announce, "[The Bureau] is successfully fulfilling the noble purpose for which it was projected."

Established in October 1862 and through September 15, 1863, the Augusta Bureau used in making clothing, 220,000 yards of woolens and 650,000 yards of cotton goods, producing 55,000 pants, 37,000 jackets, 65,000 drawers, 70,000 shirts, a complete suit costing but $20.00!

In 1863 in the field, Georgia had 44 Regiments, 7 Battalions, and 2 Companies, and were issued by the state: 5,838 hats, 43,728 jackets, 46,325 pants, 32,181 shirts, 30,068 drawers, 23,756 pairs of shoes, and 4,473 pairs of socks.

Total quantities still held by the State Quartermaster as of November, 1863: 4,719 hats, 7,291 jackets, 8,828 pants, 9,185 shirts, 8,036 drawers, 12,293 pairs of shoes, 7,517 pairs of socks, plus thousands of yards of wool, onansburgs, cotton, shoes and shoe leather, enough for several months.

Georgia would continue to clothe her own soldiers and produce the needed clothing and shoes until the fortunes of war turned Georgia into a battlefield in 1864.[2]

North Carolina

From the State of North Carolina, from October 1, 1861, through September 30, 1862, the amount of clothing manufactured or purchased, using a piece system like Georgia, was:

Items	Manufactured	Issued
Jackets	49,345	48,093
Coats	5,594	27,380
Pants	68,364	85,779
Shirts	61,275	110,723
Caps	1,288	61,949
Hats	1,192	8,918
Canteens	none	25,598
Canteen Straps	17,490	9,679
Overcoats	5,979	22,598
Brass Letters	none	6,000
Drums	8	215
Fifes	none	82
Flags	none	23 [3]

North Carolina continued to produce all clothing needed by her soldiers. In fact, after the surrender in April 1865, Governor Vance boasted that he still had 92,000 uniforms in storage. By June 1864, Colonel Dowd, Chief of the Clothing Department, announced in the papers that, "to the North Carolina Army, that there has been and is now, a sufficient quantity on hand to supply them, with the exception of shoes and blankets. As to jackets, shirts, drawers, and socks, there has been no scarcity, and if the soldiers have not been supplied, it is the fault of the brigade and regimental quartermasters."[4]

Jackson, Mississippi

From Jackson, Mississippi, before its capture in mid-1863 came, "5,000 garments a week, the material was cut and distributed all over the country to be made up by the soldiers' wives. Similar factories in Bankston, Choctaw County, Enterprise, Natchez and Woodville made up 500 a week. The hat factories in Jackson and Columbus make up 200 a week."[5]

The article stated that the output was solely for the Army of Tennessee.

South Carolina

The Graniteville, South Carolina, factory was reported in flourishing condition, turning out 16,000 yards of cloth a week in July 1862, manning 336 looms, employing 350 people, and was making plans for expanding its output.[6]

Columbus, Georgia

Columbus was established as a textile and manufacturing center long before the Civil War. The city boasted three factories. The largest, the Eagle Mills, by December 1862 was manufacturing daily 2,000 yards of heavy gray tweeds, cotton duck, and oil cloth. It was said the duck was used for tents and the oil cloth used for haversacks, etc. for the army. A quantity of stripes or ticking, osnanburgs, sheeting and knitting yarn was also produced and sold at auction daily to the local populace.

The Columbus Factory, a second textile firm, produced shirtings, osnanburgs, kerseys, and cassimeres. The Grant Factory also manufactured osnanburgs and duck material.

A letter to the Wilmington Daily Journal, in April 1863, described Columbus as:

> A perfect nest of workshops and factories. There are at least 5,000 people here living under Government employment. The Naval Iron works employ nearly 200 hands...building [steam boat] engines, and are erecting a larger rolling mill to make heavy plates for the ironclads. A German mechanic named Haiman started in a little shed making and mending swords, and now under Government contract is working 200 hands. The Ordnance Department is making large quantities of rifles and preparing all kinds of ordnance stores. The Government shoe shops are also operating on a large scale.[7]

The Columbus, Georgia, Quartermaster Depot, from records had its beginnings back in the fall of 1861. From October 1, 1861, to May 1864, the following articles came out of its shops: 305,065 pairs of shoes, 263,922 jackets, 290,092 pants, 116,146 shirts, 82,948 drawers, and 122,441 caps. The Columbus Depot was said to be the largest in the whole Confederacy, only equaled in production by the Depots in Richmond.[8]

Atlanta, Georgia

In a statement to Quartermaster-General Myers, the Atlanta Depot showed on hand, ready for issue as of March 26, 1863, 25,000 woolen jackets, 15,000 woolen pants, 65,000 shirts, 30,000 cotton drawers, 2,000 blankets, 4,000 pairs of shoes, and 3,800 wool hats. Another 90,000 yards of woolen cloth was on hand, and 135,000 yards of wool-jean material, cotton wool mix had been contracted for.

Previously out of Atlanta, from October 1862 to March 31, 1863, were manufactured 37,150 jackets, 47,390 pairs of pants, 48,692 cotton drawers, 99,720 cotton shirts, and 2,660 flannel shirts.

Major R. K. Stevenson, Quartermaster in charge of the Atlanta Depot promised if kept properly supplied with raw materials, by April 1, 1864, next year ending, he could produce 130,000 woolen jackets, 130,000 pants, 10,000 pairs of shoes, 175,000 cotton drawers, and 175,000 cotton shirts.[9]

Other depots in Macon and Athens, Georgia, Columbus, Mississippi, and Demopolis, Alabama, were also turning out uniforms, shoes, and buttons for the Quartermaster Department.

Richmond, Virginia

The *Richmond Daily Enquirer* of October 16, 1861, under their City Intelligence Column, touted the Crenshaw Woolen Company as an auxiliary, second only in importance to the Tredegar Iron Works, and the Virginia Armory, "to the success of a people engaged in an arduous struggle for their liberties."

The Crenshaw Company, established in 1860, was located next door to the Tredegar Iron Works. It manufactured, exclusively for the army, the light blue and gray cloths adopted for the regulation uniform of the Confederacy, broadcloths, and blankets. The company employed some 130 people, ran 25 broad looms, 5 sets of carding machines, and 8 spinning jacks comprising 270 spindles. By the fall of 1861, the Crenshaw Woolen Mills was producing 5,000 yards of army cloth weekly, and about 450 blankets. The blankets were said to be 60 x 80 inches in dimension, made wholly of wool, and weighed but 3.5 lbs.

The light blue color for trousers and facings produced by the mill was made possible by the receipt of an entire boatload of logwood to aid in the dyeing process received in April 1861, just days before the blockade began. Wool was obtained from local Virginia sources, as well as Texas. The cotton warp thread used in weaving army cloth was being produced in Franklinsville, North Carolina. Previously, all cotton warp was imported from England.[10]

With this volume of production, along with the increased volume of imported goods, some standardization had to be seen among the rank and file of the Provisional Army of the Confederate States. A correspondent for the *Richmond Examiner*, writing from the Army of Northern Virginia said, "It is, I humbly submit, the most agreeable news that I can communicate to the home folks, that the Army of Northern Virginia is being supplied cap-a-pie with new outfits, and I hazard to say in looks and spirits, our troops are today in nothing behind the condition of the army when it entered Pennsylvania!"[11]

An English visitor in Richmond, Virginia, a Charles Halleck, in a letter back to the *Bermuda Gazette* on September 23, 1863, wrote that the army was receiving new clothing, "Already have the motley hues of the rank and file given place in a great measure to a neat uniform of gray jackets and trousers, trousers of light blue!"

After the Battle of Kelly's Ford in November 1863, the Confederate prisoners of Hay's and Hoke's Louisiana Brigades were described as, "better clothed than we had ever seen before. All were provided with overcoats and jackets of much better material than our own. They were of English manufacture, a much darker blue than the U.S. [sky-blue overcoat], and furnished conclusive evidence of successful blockade running.[12] On November 6, 1863, a soldier of the 49th Virginia Infantry recorded in his diary, "Our troops are receiving quite a quantity of clothing and shoes. Clothing of good quality. Shoes much better than usual were being issued."[13]

The same dark clothing was mentioned by members of Jenkins' South Carolina Brigade. Private Frank M. Mixson remembered while on garrison duty in Petersburg, Virginia, that "we were given new uniforms while here and fixed up in pretty good shape." The uniforms were made, "of a cloth so dark as to be almost black. These were made of English imported blue-gray wool which at a distance, looked the same color as those worn by Northern soldiers."[14]

In the Western Theater, Sergeant Washington M. Ives, Jr., of Co. C, 4th Florida Infantry, Stovall's Brigade, wrote on October 31, 1863, that the Army of Tennessee had:

> ...drawn comfortable clothing and blankets. The coats are dark and light gray (mostly with blue collars and cuffs), the pants are light and dark gray, similar goods to the jackets, it is worsted crop between cassimere and jeans, very warm and desirable. The pants and jackets were received are of superior army goods. The caps and underclothing are miserable... quantities of new English blankets have been issued.

Ives, in a letter to his father dated January 4, 1864, was happy to report that, "the Army is still tolerably well clothed this winter, but some blankets, socks, overcoats, are much needed."[15]

An early style Georgia jacket.

Governor Brown of Georgia wanted 30,000 suits of clothing and 30,000 pairs of shoes for his volunteers that first winter of the war. A six-button jacket with two breast pockets, a dark, probably black collar, epaulettes, and cuff flashings with three buttons is pictured in many early war photos. One year later, both jackets and frock coats were sent out from state stocks. By November 1863, 40,000 suits of clothing were still on hand ready for distribution.

See also, *Military Images*, Vol. VIII, Nov.-Dec. 1986. Keith Bohannon, "More Georgians in Gray," for photos.

The Quartermaster Department increased its efforts to produce new uniforms for the troops. Inadequate transportation to move the goods would foretell a third winter of want and cold for the armies of the South.

"We were not all entirely dressed in gray uniforms."

— W.E. Matthews, 33rd Alabama.

Encamped at Shelbyville and Tullahoma, Tennessee, after fighting the Battle of Stones River, Bragg's men were in desperate need of clothing, as shown by the following description of the famous Kentucky Brigade. Hanson's men, as they marched through Murfreesboro in a heavy snowstorm were described as, "poorly shod, with poor caps, some with good jackets, many without, and none with overcoats, yet they were cheerful, and wore a proud bearing, all looked every inch men."[1] It was said that, "more than twenty men of the 6th Kentucky Regiment could not accompany their regiment being destitute of shoes."[2]

One Georgia soldier writing from camp wrote how the men, "were collecting all the produce available in middle Tennessee, and that the army has been receiving clothing and tents, although more are needed to render them comfortable."[3] He also mentioned that, "every train brings boxes of clothing for the different regiments from their folks back home."[4]

A good description of the appearance of the Army of Tennessee just before Stones River, December 31, 1862, to January 2, 1863, is given by a soldier in the 33rd Alabama Infantry:

> We were not all entirely dressed in gray uniforms; many occasionally received boxes of provisions and clothing, shoes or boots, and homemade combed wool or beaver or coon skin fur hats from folks back home, and it was quite common to see soldiers wearing home woven gray, blue, brown, or black woolen jeans pants or overcoats, gray or black homemade hats, and a majority of us wool socks sent us from home, while others wore entirely regulation gray uniform including gray cap.[5]

With clothing shortages, and a particularly cold winter for 1862-63, the Confederates were using captured Union uniforms and civilian clothing. General Braxton Bragg let his men wear any type of clothing available to them. Ironically, it was the Union commander, General Rosecrans, opposing Bragg, who took offense to Confederate soldiers wearing Federal blue, and with good reason.

That the Federal soldiers were having trouble distinguishing civilians or guerillas from regular Confederate troops brought on some very interesting dialog between U.S. Major-General Rosecrans and C. S. General Braxton Bragg. Bragg was protesting the alleged treatment of some of his regular cavalrymen as spies. The reason, according to the arresting Union officers, was the Confederates were captured in a medley of clothing, wearing anything but a full military uniform. Rosecrans suggested in a letter dated December 10, 1862, "that to prevent [any further] mistakes otherwise avoidable, it is highly desirable that your troops should at once be required to wear some badge to distinguish them from citizens."[6]

Bragg's response was the ultimate contemporary Civil War comeback. It read:

> As to your suggestion that our troops should be more particularly distinguished from citizens by a well defined uniform, I will merely state that we aim to clothe them as uniformly as the exigencies of our situation will permit. Whenever you afford us the facilities to obtain the requisite material, we shall be most happy to make the desired change. In the meantime, we shall use the best to be procured![7]

If Rosecrans wanted uniformly attired Confederates, Bragg was more than willing to take donations. Rosecrans never answered Bragg's request, but the use of Federal clothing by the Confederates brought with it a bitter side to the war.

During the Battle of Stones River, the practice of confiscating Union garments was carried on to the extreme. Confederate soldiers were stripping the dead, and more sorrowfully the wounded, of overcoats, shoes, and even their underclothing. Confederate General A.P. Stewart, commanding the Second Brigade, First Division, Polk's Corps, wrote in his official report how he was appalled at the, "plundering and stripping of the dead, even our own, and to the propriety of a general order prohibiting it."[8]

The plight of wounded Federal soldiers after the battle brought out feelings of disgust and anger in the Union ranks over their poor treatment while in the hands of the Rebels. "It is a burning shame that the enemy will pillage the dead and wounded on the field. Our men were stripped and left exposed to the terrible rains that fell during the three days of the fight."[9]

If a man were suffering from the cold, and himself in danger of succumbing to the elements, the robbing of enemy dead for their clothing is understandable. But letters and diaries of Confederate soldiers describe a more lucrative motive for robbing the dead. Scarcity of clothing that winter led to a black market trade among the C.S. camps in Tullahoma for U.S. goods and uniform items. A private in the 33rd Alabama remembered:

> There was a class of men with us who would rob the dead and did so at Murfreesboro, and men who would not entertain the thought of taking shoes off the dead themselves, but were in need of shoes and not knowing when they could get any, would pay from $10.00 to $25.00 for a second pair of brogan shoes to the man who usually said he bought them but they did not fit.

> I think all had exchanged their Enfields for Springfields on the battle fields at this time, January 1863.... We had also exchanged our cedar canteens on the battlefields or by purchase by men who had more than one cloth covered, block tin, oval shaped Yankee canteen, and those who had not picked up a U. S. blanket, good black hat, blue overcoat, or shelter tent could usually buy such cheap if needed of men who had more than one.[10]

Another Confederate soldier, one year later in December 1863, said that, "Federal overcoats were selling for $200 to $300," among the men of the 15th Arkansas Infantry of Cleburne's Division.[11]

The wearing of Union garments became so commonplace that to protect his men, General Rosecrans had printed up the following General Order No. 10, dated February 20, 1863:

> I. It having been frequently reported to the General commanding that Confederate soldiers approached our lines dressed in our uniforms, and that they have thus appeared in battle, and have thus, savage like, carried our colors to deceive us.
>
> It is ordered that none so dressed shall receive when captured, the rights of prisoners of war, and that in battle no quarter be given them. When captured singly or in squads, prowling about our lines, they shall be deemed as spies, and treated accordingly [hung].

Brigadier General U. S. Grant was experiencing a similar problem in Mississippi and issued his own General Order No. 10, on January 26, 1863. Guerillas or southern soldiers caught in the uniforms of Federal soldiers would not be treated as organized bodies of the enemy, but would be closely confined and held for the action of the War Department. Those caught within the lines of the Federal army in such uniforms or in civilian clothing would be treated as spies.

Out of the Adjutant Generals' office in Washington came General Order No. 100, the following April, stating under Section 63: "Troops who fight in the uniforms of their enemies, without any plain, striking or uniform mark of distinction of their own, can expect no quarter." Similar orders outlawing even the use of captured Federal accoutrements, unless altered in some way, were also prohibited. These restrictions were aimed primarily at the different C. S. guerillas or partisan ranger companies who did use captured Union uniforms to deceive the Federals.

Regular C.S. units were often left alone if captured in Federal garments during a major campaign or battle. One Confederate remarked:

> Nearly all the equipments of the Army of Northern Virginia were articles captured from the Yankees. Most of the blankets were marked "U.S.", also the rubber blankets or cloths. The very clothing the men wore was mostly captured, as we were allowed to wear their pants, underclothing and overcoats. As for myself, I purchased only one pair of shoes and one jacket after 1861.[12]

Yankee Dead Stripped of Clothing.

In this *Harper's Weekly* sketch, Federal soldiers bury their dead after the Battle of Fredericksburg. All the dead have been stripped of parts of their clothing, a common practice until the Battle of Murfreesboro, Tennessee, (December 31, 1862 – January 2, 1863), where even the wounded were left naked and exposed to the cold weather. This type of looting was condemned on both sides. The Confederates issued orders for their men to stay off the battlefield. The Federals issued General Order No.10, outlawing the wearing of Federal clothing by the Rebels. The penalty if caught – death.

> General Order No. 10. February 20, 1863.
>
> ORDER OF GENERAL ROSECRANS IN RELATION TO CONFEDERATE SOLDIERS WEARING YANKEE UNIFORMS.
>
> General Rosecrans has issued the following order in relation to the Confederate soldiers that may be found in Yankee uniforms:
>
> HEADQUARTERS DEP'T OF THE CUMBERLAND,
> Murfreesboro', Tenn., Feb. 20, 1863.
> [General Orders No. 10.]
>
> I. It having been frequently reported to the General Commanding that Confederate soldiers approach our lines dressed in our uniforms; and that they have appeared thus in battle, and have thus, savagelike, carried our colors to deceive us.
>
> It is ordered that none so dressed shall receive, when so captured, the rights of prisoners of war, and that, in the battle, no quarter be given them. When captured, singly or in squads, prowling about our lines, they shall be deemed as spies, and treated accordingly. The General warns all officers and men under his command to be on their guard against these violations of the rules of civilized warfare. All foraging and scouting parties, all patrols, and all troops on the march, are enjoined to arrest and examine all persons wearing our uniforms, and, if found to be wearing it without lawful authority, to forward them at once to the Provost Marshals of their commands, for indentification and investigation, and thence to the Provost Marshal General of the department, and they may be dealt with as they deserve.
>
> II. All citizens and servants wearing the United States uniform, without written permission, will be arrested, stripped, and punished according to the nature of the offence. Quartermasters will at once make requisitions for clothing to be issued to servants and employees not entitled to wear the uniform.
>
> By command of Major-General ROSECRANS.
> Official: C. Goddard, A. A. Gen. and C. of S.

Another Johnny Reb, when told he must dispense with his Yankee booty, wrote in his diary, "I'm not a spy, but some of my equipment is Federal issue. In fact, it is true for most of us. The Federal Quartermaster has furnished us supplies for a long time...we must continue to accept his generosity, for his good, [and ours]."[13]

To show what lengths some Confederates went to obtain Yankee material of war, we have Co. D of the 61st Georgia on skirmish duty. Sighting a group of Federal soldiers with some heavy knapsacks, the Georgians took after them, "As it was getting late in the Fall [October, 1863], we took after them on a run! We plundered their knapsacks till the rest of the company came up. I got two tent flies, two fine flannel overshirts, a good oilcloth, some stationary, and one of the best blankets I ever saw."[14]

Stonewall Jackson was another Confederate who regularly was able to supply and feed his men with captured Union food and clothing. So much so, that it became a joke among the Southerners. From the *Richmond Daily Dispatch*:

> Writing from the Shenandoah Valley, says a few days since a Yankee upstart belonging to Milroy's Command, summoned an aged civilian to appear before him to furnish some information. When duly arraigned, the Yankee began;
>
> Do you know any one who has furnished supplies to the Rebels?
> Old Man – I believe I do.
> Yank – Who was it?
> Old Man – General Banks.
> Yank – Sergeant, throw this man into the guardhouse! Wait a minute, do you know anyone who has been passing through our lines, and back again to the Rebels carrying information?
> Old Man – Yes, I do sir.
> Yank – Who was it?
> Old Man – Jeb Stuart!"[15]

All joking aside, some summary executions were performed on C. S. soldiers caught in Federal clothing. On January 5, 1864, Private E. S. Dodd, 8th Texas Cavalry, captured in a Federal uniform behind the lines, was hung as a spy. The threat of being shot or hung for donning the Union blue is confirmed by these soldiers who surrendered to the 60th New York Infantry in October 1863:

> A day or two after the regiment left, 37 non-commissioned officers and men of Longstreet's Corps came into Bridgeport and delivered themselves up. Deserters were numerous.
>
> The Rebels understanding that orders were given to shoot all prisoners taken having on the U.S. uniform, some laughable stories are told. When coming upon a party who find escape impossible, the first thing they usually discover is U. S. clothing scattered along the road, and when captured some are entirely destitute of covering in fear of the consequences."[16]

From this, it would be historically accurate at any late war period reenactments to have Confederates captured in their underwear or butt naked. The crowd would love it. Living history in the buff!

Historical references exist in Confederate letters and diaries to Federal clothing being altered. Union overcoats and pants which were a light blue colored wool were easily re-dyed, and sometimes

Sergeant Henry T. Wright. Co. E. 61st Georgia.

Sergeant Wright appears well equipped and clothed for the campaigns of 1862. By 1863, the Confederates from necessity were using the captured clothing and accoutrements of the Federal Army. Some men of his regiment in chased a group of Yankee soldiers they spotted with fat knapsacks. Sergeant Wright was captured at Spotsylvania Courthouse on May 12, 1864, and spent the rest of the war in a Yankee prison. Leighton Young

the buttons were removed and C. S. issue buttons were substituted. A common method for dying in the field was to soak the clothing in an oozing vat of water stained with walnut hulls, butternut bark, coffee, or rusty iron. A shade of brown from mustard to cinnamon would be the result.

"The Confederate soldier is forced to resort to many expedients to obtain clothing," wrote a member of Calvert's Battery, Alabama Light Artillery, Army of Tennessee. "I have been employed this day in coloring a Yankee overcoat, which I brought from the battlefield of Missionary Ridge."[17]

General Nathan Bedford Forrest, in December 1864, forbade his men to wear captured clothing unless it was altered in some fashion. Forrest issued a General Order stating that those soldiers in whose possession was found un-dyed clothing, would have the garment taken from them, and turned back into the Quartermaster![18]

A cavalryman of the 2nd Kentucky, Morgan's Command, remembered capturing some blue Union overcoats at Hartsville, Tennessee, and that they, "were dyed black and worn by our men afterward."[19] One Confederate captured at Missionary Ridge spoke of, "good rations," but "everything resembling Yankee uniforms was taken from us." He felt this type of behavior on the part of his captors, "a little harsh." Whatever the consequences, the use of Federal accoutrements and garments continued to the end of the War.[20]

"Well clad and armed, tolerably well shod."

— Col. Wm. P. Johnston, Insp. Gen'l.

The continued reports of ragged clothing and bare feet among the rank and file of the Army of Tennessee, along with a growing dissension in the officer ranks against General Bragg, brought from the War Department a specially appointed Inspector General. Colonel William Preston Johnston, Aide-de-Camp to President Jefferson Davis himself, was given the job to investigate, "the [Western Armies] means of procuring supplies, and the condition of the Army in general."

Arriving at the headquarters of the Army at Tullahoma, Colonel Johnston witnessed a review of Hardee's Corp on March 23, 1863, Brigadier General B. R. Johnson's Brigade the same day, the Kentucky Brigade on March 24, and Polk's Corp at Shelbyville on March 30. Colonel Johnston was singularly impressed with Wither's Division of Polk's Corp, whom he described as, "principally Mississippians" and, "the best clad I saw in the Army."[1]

In a conversation with a Major M. B. McMiken, acting Chief Quartermaster of the Army, McMiken commented:

> ...the army was fully supplied with clothing, and had some 6,000 suits in its depot [in Chattanooga]. Shoes were the most desperately needed article in the Army. A requisition for some 10,000

pairs was made, but not yet filled. It was also brought up that the uniforms now being issued to the men were of a "much better material" than the uniforms during the winter of 1861-62.[2]

A review of Liddell's Brigade, Hardee's Division on June 1, 1863, showed the men to be, "well clothed", but still, "without any attempt at uniformity in color or cut, but nearly all were dressed in gray or brown coats and felt hats."[3] Sir Arthur Fremantle, as part of the reviewing staff, was told of the un-uniform appearance of the men that, "even if a regiment was clothed in proper uniform by the Government, it would become parti-colored again in a week. The soldiers preferred wearing the coarse homespun jackets and trousers made by their mothers and sisters back home."[4]

Fremantle continued with, "most of the officers were dressed in a uniform which is neat and serviceable — a blueish gray frock coat of a color similar to Austrian Yagers. The infantry wear blue facings, the artillery red, the doctors black, the staff white, and the cavalry yellow." On their weapons, "most of them were armed with Enfield rifles captured from the enemy. As to bayonets, an observation was made that, "many had lost or thrown away their bayonets, which they don't appear to value properly, as they assert that they never met any Yankee who would wait for that weapon."[5]

Bayonets had been ordered from the Selma Arsenal, but the supply available, if able to be filled at all, was hampered by the lack of machinery and skilled workmen. In his report to President Davis, Major Johnston blamed the loss of bayonets, "over on-half of the [armies] missing, to the shortness of the scabbards!"[6]

Lieutenant Colonel Oladowski, the ordnance officer attached to the Army of Tennessee, put the blame squarely on the soldiers by saying, "the arms, accoutrements, and ammunition in the hand of the [troops] on the march are carelessly wasted." Oladowski wanted to see the commanders of companies held responsible for the loss of often times irreplaceable arms and accoutrements, as the only way, "the evil can be corrected."[7]

All things considered, Major Johnston found the Army of Tennessee, "well clad and armed, tolerably well shod, and marked with every evidence of good discipline and courage."[8]

On June 24, 1863, the quiet camp life of the Army came to an end, as General Rosecrans began his campaign to push Bragg out of Tennessee. It was called the Tullahoma Campaign, and in a se-

---

Soldiers' Clothing.
From the Alabama Beacon, July 24, 1863.
(Extract from a circular address of Governor Shorter of July 13, 1863, to the people of Alabama.)

The state has not been unmindful of the claims upon her attention, of her brave soldiers, who, far away from their homes, are risking their lives in her defense. Every provision in her power has been made for their comfort. The returns of the quartermaster's department show that the following quantity and kind of clothing have been furnished them since my inauguration: 11,723 hats, 3373 overcoats, 14,870 jackets, 16,220 pants, 31,784 shirts, 16,876 drawers, 10,569 pairs of socks, 16,960 pairs of shoes, and 2384 blankets. These articles have been supplied at cost and charges and at one-half the price for which they could have been obtained from other hands. Besides clothing issued to the camps, the state has furnished large quantities of hospital stores of every description, for the use and comfort of her sick and wounded soldiers. No state has made better provision for her troops, and no state has been more highly honored by the gallant deeds of her sons than Alabama.

Wither's Division of Polk's Corps, Shelbyville, Tennessee, March 30, 1862.

The Special Inspector to the Army of Tennessee was impressed with the military appearance of Wither's Division of Polk's Corps calling them, "the best clad I saw in the Army." Two brigades of the division were Mississippians, but several Alabama regiments made up the difference. How were these troops dressed? The Alabama regiments, from this newspaper article, were getting uniforms from their state.

Lee White

---

ries of quick flanking movements, Rosecrans caused Bragg to retreat all the way back to Chattanooga. On August 21, Rosecrans moved again. Outflanked and unsure of Rosecran's position, Bragg abandoned Chattanooga on September 18, 1863. He retreated south to the area around Chickamauga Creek and Lafayette, Tennessee. It was here, near Lee and Gordon's Mill, that Bragg, now heavily reinforced from Mississippi and soon Virginia, awaited the Federal advance.

Battle of Chickamauga, September 19-20, 1863.

Uniform descriptions from Chickamauga, like Stones River, are unfortunately few, or yet undiscovered, but Longstreet's Corps, just arrived from the Army of Northern Virginia, stood in sharp contrast to the soldiers of the Army of Tennessee. Longstreet's men were issued new uniforms in Virginia, described as:

> ...dark blue [gray] round jacket, closely fitting, with light-blue trousers, which made a line of Confederates resemble that of the enemy, the only difference being the cut of the garments — the Federals wearing a loose blouse instead of a jacket. The uniforms of the Eastern troops [Longstreet's], made quite a contrast with the tattered and worn jeans of their Western brethren.[9]

Bragg's Westerners were described by Longstreet's men as generally, "greasy, dirty, raggedy, barefooted, and wearing go-as-you-please . . .with every imaginable variety of garments and head covering."[10]

C. S. General Moxley Sorrell, Longstreet's Chief of Staff, in his memoirs made mention of a Western tunic used by the Army of Tennessee. Whether this refers to their gray jackets with the blue collar and cuffs issued from the Columbus Depot or possibly an overshirt of some sort, is not known. It is known that in contrast to Longstreet's men at Chickamauga, the soldiers of the Army of Tennessee were un-uniform in dress.[11]

In the two day battle of Chickamauga, September 19 - 20, 1863, Rosecrans was forced to retreat to Chattanooga and the Union forces were put under siege by Bragg's Army. The following month of October was devoted to strengthening the Confederate positions around Chattanooga, primarily Missionary Ridge and Lookout Mountain, with the hope that the Union forces would be starved into surrendering.

During the winter months of 1863 and into the spring of 1864 came the distribution of thousands of new uniforms, hats, caps, shoes and blankets to the soldiers of the Army of Tennessee. From letters and diaries, the Government clothing was of a better quality, material and color than issued the year before. "Our regiment is drawing some excellent clothing," wrote a soldier in Bates' Brigade, "jackets of gray, blue cuffs, pants, shoes, caps, etc." Bragg's ragged veterans found their new clothes, "comely [and] pleasant, which makes a good uniform and satisfies a soldier."[12]

As was the case generally in the Confederate Army, not all would receive or accept new clothing from the Quartermaster. Like Stones River nine months earlier, those who were the most destitute

---

Longstreet's Corps at Chickamauga, "We drew new uniforms as we passed through Richmond."

We know that Longstreet's Corps was sent west in September 1863 to reinforce Bragg's Army of Tennessee. They arrived by train wearing new Richmond Quartermaster Depot uniforms. Corporal Wm. A. Brown of Stanford's Mississippi Battery, remembered that on the morning of September 19, 1863:

> We passed the Virginia troops who had come to reinforce us for the coming fight. Our first impression on seeing them was that they were Yankees! This impression was caused partly by the color of their uniforms, but more by its uniformity, and the superior style of their equipments, in haversacks, canteens, and knapsacks. The contrast between them and General Bragg's motley ragged troops, was striking in the extreme. If this command was a specimen of Lee's troops, they are certainly superior to the Army of Tennessee in dress!

Another Army of Tennessee veteran, Captain Frank T. Ryan of the 1st Arkansas Mounted Rifles, was surprised even more by the style and color of uniform worn by Longstreet's soldiers. Ryan and his company took cover, having advanced too far in front of their brigade:

> When we learned the dangerous situation of ourselves we halted. In the mean time, the troops in our rear were coming steadily towards us...some insisted they were Longstreet's men and therefore our friends, others said they could distinquish them plainly and they were Federals. How such a difference of opinion could arise was owing to how Longstreet's men were uniformed. They wore light blue pants, gray jackets, and regular soldiers caps. We, on the other hand, the Western troops had no uniform at all, but wore clothes of all kinds and hues.

The jacket and cap color was described as, "dark steel gray, the same color and fabric worn by our officers." Consensus among researchers is that these jackets and caps were made of imported English cloth of a darker blue-gray shade.

By mid-December 1863, two months later, this uniform was reduced to rags. Longstreet's men had to wait another five months before a second issue of clothing came to them.

General Hood is wounded at Chicamauga.

This Vizetelly sketch from the *Illustrated London News*, Vol. XLIII, Dec. 26, 1863, depicts the wounding of General John Bell Hood amid his Texas Brigade at Chickamauga. Vizetelly was an eyewitness to the event and drew Hood's Texans in short jackets, blanket rolls, and some in caps with a light colored band. The uniform color of Longstreets's Texans might have caused Hood to be shot by his own soldiers. Captain Todd of Co. A, 1st Texas, recalled on the morning of the 20th of September:

> Our Regiment and the 4th Texas advanced so far in front of Bragg's lines, that with our new uniforms looking blue, we drew the fire of our men in the rear and caused some confusion.... Here also General Hood rode up and took the flag of the 4th Texas to rally them under this rear fire, when he himself, was shot again, and then lost his leg.... This scribe saw this and believes the bullet from our own men struck him.

Unidentifed Confederate in gray jacket and light blue trousers.

This tinted tintype shows a soldier wearing a Richmond Depot type II jacket and light blue trousers. Light blue trousers in great numbers were issued to both armies throughout the fall and winter of 1863-1864. The light blue color was dropped by the Confederates in August 1864. The reason? Too many Southern soldiers were getting shot while wearing dark jackets and light blue pants because they looked like Yankees!

Mr. James Dews

❖ Middle War Period, October 1862 – November 1864 ❖

or threadbare searched the battlefield of Chickamauga for Yankee or Confederate clothing. If they could not find what they needed, there were those soldiers around who had shoes or hats for sale or barter. A soldier in the 15th Texas Infantry inspected the work of the scavengers and found, "many [of the dead] had been stripped of all clothing, and many whose pockets had been rifled and turned out," just after the battle.[13] After the scavengers came the Army Quartermaster and Ordnance Officers who sent out details to police the field, gathering up, "abandoned guns, accoutrements, even taking the harness of the dead horses, and other war stores scattered about," observed one of Bragg's men.[14]

During the siege of Chattanooga, rations were reported as short and of inferior quality. There was no soap, which meant the new clothing would not last but a few months. Boiling uniforms in hot water to kill lice was all a poor soldier could do for cleanliness.[15] The officers of the Army of Tennessee suffered right along with the men, if not more so. Their ability to keep themselves properly uniformed and fed brought some needed changes out of Richmond.

"An Officer's uniform out here costs three-hundred and fifty dollars and it's impossible to get a good one."

— Lt. J. W. Harris, Army of Tennessee.

While the privates in the army were able to draw clothing from the quartermaster, their officers were finding it difficult to maintain an appearance befitting their rank. A scarcity of fine gray wool, a scandal out of Richmond over the illicit sale of Government cloth, and the resulting General Order ending the sales of cloth to officers until their men were supplied, led to some embarrassing situations among the upper echelons of the army.

The Inspector-General of Vaughn's Brigade, John W. Harris, in a letter home to Memphis, Tennessee, confided to a friend that, "we can't get a suit of clothes out here [Chattanooga] for less than four-hundred dollars, and with our small pay, it is an impossibility for us to even save that much."[1] Harris wanted to borrow fifty dollars to be given to his mother in Memphis to buy him, "a pair of navy blue pants with lace stripes." Harris promised his friend that the favor would not go un-rewarded, and that he would someday pay him back for his troubles.

The officers of Bate's Brigade, feeling the pinch like Harris, felt the time was at hand to draft a resolution to the Confederate Congress detailing their plight. The resolution stated that in consequence of high prices [inflation and speculation], the officers could no longer afford rations for their messes, "and that it has become impossible for regimental and line officers, especially subalterns, to subsist and clothe themselves out of the pay allowed by the Government."[2]

A schedule of prices that accompanied the resolution showed that the average cost for a tailored officer's regulation frock coat was $350, a pair of boots $250, pants $125, hat $80 to $125, shirts $50, drawers $15, and socks $10 for late 1863, totaling around $980 to $1000 for a uniform when the monthly pay for a 2nd Lieutenant was $80 a month. One well-to-do Confederate officer remarked how a new uniform, complete, set him back over $1700, an impossible sum of money for most junior officers to come up with.

On March 4, 1864, as a remedy, General Order Number 28. was passed out of Richmond, stating that:

> All commissioned officers of the armies of the Confederate States shall be allowed to purchase clothing and cloth for clothing, from any quartermaster, at the price which it cost the Government, all expenses included, and that they are now entitled to one ration in kind, each in kind and quality the same now allowed by law to privates.

It was further stated that, "no quartermaster was allowed to issue clothing and cloth which would be a proper issue to privates, until all privates...have been fully supplied." This stipulation did not sit too well with some Confederate officers. One was General Hardee, then Commander of the Army of Tennessee, who was refused the sale of cloth for a new uniform because his men were not fully uniformed.

A special Congressional committee was selected to look into the matter of officers' clothing. It was reported that in the latter half of 1864, 31,940 yards of fine cloth were furnished through the

Quartermaster Department. An unreasonably large proportion of this material was found to be going to those officers serving in rear echelon duties, some 14/15th of the total issued. Why only 1/15th was going to the field officers was questioned by the Committee, but no satisfactory explanation could be found. The location and availability of the material to those officers serving near the depot in Richmond was the only answer. The field officers were unable to obtain the cloth while on campaign, and no provisions were made by the depots in getting it to the front.[3] The amount of officers' grade cloth carried in the depots was also found to be inadequate.

Quartermaster Lawton countered with, "1,000 suits are being made up here [Montgomery, Ala.] for the officers of Lee's command, and that provision has been made for over 6,000 officers in the past six months, [Fall, 1864]." Officers' uniforms were now being supplied from the Quartermaster Department.[4]

Many officers chose to have their uniforms sent from home or were drawing enlisted men clothing instead. Homespun butternut or gray jeans officer's frocks began to appear at parades and on the battlefield. The following description of a group of some 460 captured Confederate officers illustrates the diversity in uniforms being worn:

> There among them were tall, lank mountaineers, dark, long-haired and fierce of aspect, and a lesser number of city men of jauntier appearance. The major part were common looking, evidentially of the poorer class of Southerners, with a spreading of foreigners, principally Germans and Irish. Hardly any two dressed alike. They wore suits of blue jeans, homespuns of butternut, and a few in costumes of gray more or less trimmed. Upon their heads were all sorts of covering, straw and slouch hats, and forage caps of gray, blue, or red, decorated with braid. Cavalry boots, shoes, and bootees, in all stages of wear on their feet. Their effects were wrapped in rubber sheets, pieces of carpet, or parts of quilts and comforts. Some had sacks of ancient make. Haversacks of waterproof cloth and cotton hung from their shoulders.[5]

Another change in officers' uniforms was noted in the *Wilmington Daily Journal* of April 3, 1863. It seems that the white and buff facings on some coats, "were easily soiled, and so difficult to clean [were] fast going out of use. In defiance of the regulations our officers were having their coats made plain without any facings."[6]

**Alexander Robert Lawton, {1818-1896}
2nd Quartermaster General of the Confederacy.**

Alexander Lawton was born on November 4, 1818, to a wealthy, influential planter family from South Carolina. Lawton graduated from West Point in 1839, resigning his commission in the artillery in 1841. He studied law at Harvard University, set up practice in Savannah, Georgia, married, and employed himself in several business ventures. Elected to the Georgia state legislature in 1855, he adopted a staunch pro-slavery platform. When the Civil War came, Lawton became colonel of the 1st Volunteer Georgia Infantry. In 1862, he left for Virginia and served with the Army of Northern Virginia until wounded at Antietam.

Appointed Quartermaster General on August 7, 1863, by his friend Jefferson Davis, Lawton was reluctant to take the job. The man he was replacing, Abraham Myers, had many supporters in the Confederate Congress, and in the presidential cabinet. He was confronted with a shortage of both shoes and clothing for the army. On October 13, he made the statement, "the Depots are quite bare." Future prospects looked bleak.

Lawton suffered the same complaints and persecution as Myers. His department was investigated by a special Congressional Committee in December 1864, and although exonerated of all charges, Lawton still took the blame for the bare-feet and rags of the last campaigns of the war.

> "Shoes, Shoes, Shoes! the Army needs shoes!" *The Daily Journal*, Wilmington, North Carolina, June 9, 1863.
>
> While many of our noble soldiers are barefooted, we see it stated that 7,000 lbs. of government leather was destroyed by Averill at Salem. What was this leather doing there?
>
> While many of the Georgia troops in Bragg's Army were reported shoeless, the Quartermaster of the State announces that he has as many as 3,000 pairs of shoes. What were they doing in Atlanta, when a few hours travel could have carried them to the sufferers? — *Savannah Republican.*
>
> They are saving the shoes for seeds of course!? We are surprised that a journal usually conducted with so much intelligence, as is exhibited in the columns of the Republican, should ask such a question and should know that shoes and other army supplies are stored carefully by the quartermaster and other depositories to be kept and to be destroyed in case of a grand movement, called retreat or evacuation. They have a Governor in North Carolina indeed, who imported shoes and clothing and issued supplies immediately to the soldiers—but that was in North Carolina. — *Charleston Courier.*

Inflation, cloth shortages, General Orders, and dirty uniforms would all have an effect on the appearance of the staff and field officers of the Confederacy. In the last year of the war it was difficult to distinguish the officers from the privates in the Confederate Army.

"A panic which I never before witnessed, seemed to have seized on both officers and men."

— Major General Braxton Bragg

Lookout Mountain, Missionary Ridge.

If Confederate General Braxton Bragg ever had a chance to inflict a staggering defeat on a Union Army, it was Union General Rosecrans' Army of the Cumberland, bottled up in Chattanooga. Rosecrans' men were short of food, ammunition, clothing, and fuel to keep warm. The possibility of a retreat by Rosecrans was the cause for his being relieved of command. He was replaced by General George H. Thomas, who was ordered to hold "at all hazards," and informed that General U. S. Grant was on the way. Grant arrived in Chattanooga on October 22, 1863.

In a campaign almost as spectacular as Vicksburg, Grant in one month's time broke the siege, established a supply line, reinforced the garrison, and attacked Bragg's forces. The Battles of Lookout Mountain on November 24, and Missionary Ridge on November 25, cost the Confederates 4,100 to 6,100 soldiers, thousands of small arms, and 31 pieces of artillery.

The Rebel retreat was that of a demoralized army. Infantryman Peter McClain of the 84th Illinois made note of what was left behind by the Johnnies as they abandoned the Chattanooga area: "We started on the road towards Ringgold, Georgia. As the rebels were retreating towards Dalton, we went along slowly, and could see on the road evidence the Rebels were in quite a hurry. They left wagons, gun carriages, tents, blankets, old pieces of carpeting, in fact anything to lighten their load and aid their flight."[1]

The Confederate prisoners were described as, "tolerably well-clothed, though not in uniform, and the majority well provided with blankets." Even with thousands of new jackets, trousers, and caps distributed, the men still looked un-uniform by military standards.[2]

Bragg's army ended their retreat at Dalton, Georgia. Bragg, greatly depressed with his defeat at Missionary Ridge, penned his resignation on November 30, 1863. General William Hardee was given temporary command on December 2.

General Hardee went to work to revive the Army of Tennessee. Reinforcements were requested and sent, rations became more plentiful, needed forage was found for the animals, and most importantly to the men, a system of furloughs was ordered to keep up morale.

Quartermaster's stores, blankets, overcoats, and especially shoes were in short supply. As an aide, Hardee ordered many of his Georgia and Alabama troops home to bring back warm clothing for themselves and their comrades. A soldier in the 33rd

Three Confederate Officers, two in plain frock coats, one in regulation.

The first officer, a major, though properly dressed, by 1864 might have requisitioned a private's uniform for field use, and put his uniform in storage. The two other officers are dressed in non-regulation uniforms. The difficulty and expense of obtaining a Confederate officer's uniform of fine grade wool cloth with gold trimmings resulted in the officers of Bate's Brigade drafting a resolution to the Confederate Congress explaining their plight. USAMHI

Alabama Infantry wrote how important these furloughs and resulting packages were regarded by both officers and men:

> Often when a man returned home to camp, he would take charge of boxes and provisions, clothing and shoes sent to the boys in camp by relatives, and would have to stay with the boxes on freight cars while his leave of absence had expired.
>
> One time, [a Private Faulk of Co. K] was more than two weeks getting from Eufala to camp with our boxes. However, he was not punished for absence without leave![3]

General Hardee, when offered command of the Army, declined for personal reasons. General Polk was given temporary command on December 23, and finally General Joseph E. Johnston was selected as the most likely choice to succeed Bragg. Johnston took over formally on December 27, 1863.

In an interesting letter to General Johnston from Confederate President Jefferson Davis, Davis assured Johnston that the Army of Tennessee was not as bad off in terms of supplies as believed after Missionary Ridge. The artillery, having lost some 41 guns, was reported, "well-supplied with horses and equipments, with enough guns [112] still left, sufficient for the strength of the army." Less than fifty wagons and ambulances had been lost or captured, and the livestock appeared to be in generally good condition. Small arms could be easily replaced; 20,000 smooth-bore muskets were in storage in Atlanta and elsewhere. Ammunition was no problem, and was even said to be in abundance. The soldiers themselves, "were tolerably provided with clothing, and a heavy shipment of shoes and blankets was expected daily."[4]

In a January 2, 1864, reply to Davis, Johnston found the Army encamped around Dalton, "not entirely recovered [in] its confidence." The men were, "generally comfortably clothed, but a few shoes and blankets were wanting in each brigade." The artillery was "sufficient," but Johnston added, "[lacking] in discipline and instruction."[5]

Johnston, after conducting a more thorough inspection of the Army two weeks later, found an even greater deficiency in shoes and blankets that expected. Johnston remarked how, "painful it was for him, to see the number of bare feet in every regiment." He found two of the four brigades reviewed that day, "not in a condition to march for want of shoes!"[6] A Texas soldier in Cleburne's Division summed it up this way:

> I am more poorly clad at this time [December 24, 1863], than I ever was at any previous period [of the war]. Our money is so depreciated that it will not purchase what we want. I have money plenty...but cannot find good articles of clothing for the winter. The troops are rather poorly clad, wanting shoes and socks very much, and the prospect of getting them is rather slim.[7]

"The Depots are quite bare."

— Q. M. Gen'l. Lawton

Lawton, in a letter to a Mr. Colin J. McRae, special loan agent and financial manager of Confederate accounts overseas, needed the release of more monies or credits immediately for the Quartermaster Department. Lawton himself expressed, "a great anxiety" over the ability of his department to supply, "indispensable articles of clothing, such as shoes, blankets, and overcoats." His depots and the Southern marketplace were empty. The Southern people themselves were as destitute and hungry, in some cases, as the soldiers.[1]

Supply shortages of the winter of 1863-64 go all the way back to the spring of 1863. Quartermaster General Myers had made arrangements overseas for enough imported items he felt adequate to supplement the government depot production. The atmosphere around the Department smacked of confidence in its ability to meet all demands for the fall of 1863. No more rags and barefeet this winter. The post-Antietam clothing scandal would not occur again.

Everything would change when two Q.M. contract steamers, the Hebe, and the Venus, were lost off Wilmington in September and October 1863. Lawton quoted the loss of shoes alone at 100,000 pairs. Lawton, now under pressure from all fronts, promised President Davis that 600,000 pairs of shoes would be ready in two months' time, if everything he was working on went according to plan.[2]

By September 1863, the depots were indeed empty. The massive requisitions for all types of clothing for Robert E. Lee's Army of Northern Virginia, and Braxton Bragg's Army of Tennessee, besides every other soldier in the Confederacy, had cleaned out government stocks.

Lee had been complaining for weeks on the poor condition of his men, without shoes and clothing. In a response dated October 12, 1863, Lawton said he had just sent to the A.N.V. a total of 10,000 pairs of shoes. 2,000 were from Richmond, 1,229 from Wilmington, 3,500 from Columbus, Georgia, which Lee said were poor quality, and 3,000 from Lee's own shoe shop, which Lee had overlooked. Another 10,500 pairs of imported shoes and 6,500 blankets were sent out having just arrived through the blockade at Wilmington. All types of clothing, Lawton said, were now in fair supply in Richmond, "and other depots."[3]

For the Army of Tennessee, 12,000 blankets were being held in storage at Atlanta. In September 1863, Bragg's army was supplied with new clothing. Chief Quartermaster Dillard at the Columbus, Georgia, depot informed Richmond, "[in filling the requisitions] for Bragg's army and [the Department of Mississippi and Louisiana], have entirely run me out of stock for the present." The Columbus Depot, one of the largest in the Confederacy, by late September 1863 was temporarily out of quartermaster goods.[4] General Joseph E. Johnston, in trying to get new clothing for his forces in the Department of Mississippi and Louisiana, inquiring as to what was available in his district, was informed that, "Major Mims, [Jackson, Mississippi Depot] reports no blankets or tents, few shoes; 3,000 suits of clothing. Major Winnemore [Augusta, Georgia Depot] reports neither blankets nor other clothing. Major Calhoun [Montgomery, Alabama Depot] the same. Can we be furnished with these things from somewhere else?"[5]

Lawton, by pulling some departmental strings, was able to procure for Johnston 8,000 uniforms and 7,000 pairs of shoes out of Colum-

Blankets for the Confederacy.

An essential piece of equipment for any Civil War soldier was a good, warm blanket. Wool blankets, by 1862, were in short supply. By necessity, old quilts, and those made of carpeting or jeans cloth were used instead. The woven cotton carpeting used in Southern homes was cut up and sent to the soldiers as donations. Carpet blankets were also manufactured by the Quartermaster Department. An 1863 ledger entry for the Atlanta Depot stated 20,559 yards of carpeting were in storage for making blankets.

The State Quartermaster of Georgia, Ira R. Foster, was using jeans for making up blankets in 1864:

> In my last report I referred to the impossibility of purchasing blankets in the Confederacy.... I was ordered soon after by the Governor to have manufactured at the earliest possible moment, out of jeans and kersies lined with shirting, 10,000 blankets which order was promptly filled. During the year I have also received three bales of English blankets, which were run through the blockade and all are on hand for the coming winter requisitions.

From October 15, 1863, to October 15, 1864, Georgia sent out 4,229 jeans blankets and had 4,895 on hand, plus the English blankets.

A Carpet blanket.

Courtesy Pat Kline – Family Heirloom Weavers.

bus, Georgia, along with a few thousand blankets and tents. Lawton informed Johnston further on September 26, that the Atlanta Depot had 1,700 pairs of shoes, 12,000 blankets, and a "large lot of clothing [except pants] on hand," if he wanted them. Some quartermaster stores did arrive, but Major A.M. Barbous, Chief Quartermaster for Johnston, reported that by October 5, 1863, "the supplies furnished upon your orders were very meager and the shoes have not all arrived yet," and would not arrive for months![6]

In a letter writing campaign, Johnston informed President Davis things down here were not so good. "The want of shoes is painful to see even in this mild weather. Although the Chief Quartermaster [Lawton] promised when I arrived [in Dalton] to supply the deficiency, only 4,200 pairs of shoes were received by January, 1864, not more than a fourth of the number necessary to supply the monthly wear."[7]

Lawton, in response, wrote, "that a full share of the supply on command was being shipped to Johnston as quickly as possible." Lieutenant F. W. Sims of the Confederate States Railroad Bureau, informed Lawton that out of Atlanta, "bountiful supplies for General Johnston's army of everything but long forage, is going forward in considerable quantities."[8]

For the spring of 1864, besides government stocks, the Army of Tennessee received thousands of uniforms from private sources. An estimated 5,000 - 7,000 full uniforms came out of the Georgia Soldier's Bureau, and another 10,000 - 20,000 were sent out west from North Carolina, by Governor Vance. Vance was distributing state overstocks of clothing to some of his favorite officers. Luckily, some of his favorites were in the Army of Tennessee.[9]

The Augusta Soldier's Bureau, Georgia's own Quartermaster Department, had distributed 15,000 uniforms and 30,000 pairs of shoes to all the armies that winter, and 3,000 new uniforms, complete, were sent to the Georgia troops in Longstreet's Corp encamped at Morriston, East Tennessee. What little Georgia did send to Longstreet came none too soon, as Longstreet's men were reduced to begging for anything that could keep them warm and fed.

PART NINE

"Greater suffering and privation than anything experienced...during the whole struggle."

— Maj. Winkler, 4th Texas Inf.

If there ever was a tale of woe, cold, and hunger amongst the Confederate rank and file, it was that suffered by Longstreet's little army during the Knoxville campaign in the winter of 1863-64.

On November 4, 1863, General Longstreet with his two divisions, plus Joe Wheeler's calvary and Colonel Alexander and Leyden's artillery, a total of 15,000 men, were ordered to drive out or capture Union General Burnside's Army at Knoxville, Tennessee. The attack was to be swift and secret, but from the very start was doomed to fail. Everything from wagons, artillery, horses, sustenance, clothing, maps, guides, and especially shoes, were just not available or in poor condition.

Brigadier General J. B. Robertson of the Texas Brigade was brought up on charges stemming from his open complaint against such an expedition. He declared:

> that our men were in no condition for campaigning; that General Longstreet had promised shoes, but how could they be furnished?; that we only just had communication with Richmond, and could not even get mail from there in less than three weeks; that he [Robertson] was opposed to the movement, and that he would require written orders to move, and would only obey them under protest![1]

Captain Frank Potts, Assistant Q.M., Longstreet's Corps, referred to the wagons and animals given him for the campaign as the, "worst I ever saw." Potts recalled how his, "wagons frequently broke down...the mules just able to carry their harness, the harnesses much worn, and many teams [were found] without collars or saddles," making it difficult for the teams to pull or the drivers to control the mules.[2]

The situation became so bad, the Confederates were collecting the carcasses of dead mules and horses being thrown into the Holston River for their horseshoes and nails. Oxen were impressed to help pull the caissons of Leyden's artillery. Two other batteries, a total of four guns, had to be left behind. There were few good horses and too many guns.

Obtaining enough food for the troops became a dire problem. When the expedition started, Major R. J. Moses, Chief Commissary, reported that the command upon leaving Tyner's Station by rail, "were without meat rations." Rations were said to be waiting for them in Sweetwater, but through some misunderstanding were sent back to Chickamauga Station. Moses was dumbfounded. "The troops were without meat, and no provision whatever had been made for their supplies."[3]

From the time Longstreet left Chattanooga on November 4, until they abandoned the siege of Knoxville on December 2, the commissary was never able to accumulate more than a two-day supply of food. The greater portion of it came from foraging parties. Moses commented that some of the men were without flour rations for, "[sometimes a week], and supplies did not become regular until the Army reached the rail head at Morristown three days later, December 5."[4]

A shortage of shoes was extremely hard on the soldiers. The weather the first week in November had turned bitterly cold, and the ground and roads were frozen hard. Sharp angles from the wagon ruts and ice patches cut the men's feet. Colonel Alexander wrote, "I myself had seen bloody stains on the frozen ground, left by the barefooted where our infantry had passed."[5] Both Longstreet and his chief of staff, Col. Moxley Sorrel, recalled "the bloody marks in the road." Sorrel estimated that 2,000 were totally without shoes, and the rest near to it.[6]

The soldiers began to fashion what they called Longstreet's moccasins, sandals made out of rawhide from slaughtered cattle. Some in Kershaw's Brigade resorted to wrapping their feet in pieces of blankets. In the artillery, those who rode the caissons gave their shoes to the cannoneers who had to walk.[7] General Longstreet gave his permission for the men to swap shoes with Yankee prisoners. The conditions were that a genuine swap was to take place, each man to have something to trade, and not leave the prisoner barefoot.[8]

Rail service with Richmond was not completed until January 26, 1864. In the interim, besides taking the shoes and clothing off Yankee prisoners, a shoe shop was started while the Army was encamped in Morristown, Tennessee. From Longstreet's memoirs:

> **"Joe Brown Clothes."** Ira Foster and the State of Georgia sent 3,000 uniforms to Longstreet's Georgia Brigades, March 1864.
>
> In order to receive clothing from the State of Georgia, an officer had to fill out the following application:
>
> I certify, on honor, that there are _____ non-commisioned officers and privates to the _____ Georgia Vol's. present, and that _____ of them are destitute of the articles called for, which they cannot otherwise procure; and that I have repeated efforts to draw from the Confederate Government, but failed to secure the adequate supply.
>
> The 16th Georgia Infantry was issued the following items: 23 blankets, 55 coats, 52 pants, 32 drawers, 33 shirts, 63 prs. of shoes, and 33 pairs of socks. Every Georgia regiment in Longstreet's Corps received part of the total donation. From the issue numbers, the clothing went to those most in need. The color of the uniform was described as a, "dingie white." From the State Quartermaster's Report the cloth used was, "colored osnaburg."
>
> Foster also commented that private contracts for wool uniforms were made in 1864, and that enough wool had been procured to begin making up uniforms of a kersey, cotton wool mix.
>
> Annual Report of Ira R. Foster, Quartermaster General of Georgia. For the fiscal year ending October 15, 1864. Milledgeville, GA. 1864. (Courtesy of Lee White); Heller, J. R. & C. A. Eds., *The Confederacy is on her way up the spout: Letters to South Carolina, 1861-1864*. Athens, Georgia: The University of Georgia Press, 1992, 116.

The Augusta Soldier's Bureau donated another 3,000 uniforms and shoes for the Georgia soldiers of Longstreet's Corps. A letter of thanks was returned on March 22, 1864, to Georgia's own quartermaster, Colonel Ira R. Foster, as the clothing came at a time when the men's needs were the greatest.[11]

Longstreet's East Tennessee campaign ended on December 23, 1863, with little to show for the effort. Longstreet had to abandon the Knoxville siege on December 2, with the news of Bragg's defeat at Missionary Ridge and his ensuing retreat to Dalton, Georgia. Longstreet chose to retreat himself toward Virginia, with the hope of punishing the enemy somewhere else. Three missed opportunities at Lenoir's Station on November 16, Campbell's Station on November 17, and Bean's Station on December 13-15, deprived him of the captured spoils he needed so badly. The arrival of cold weather forced him into winter camp.

Longstreet, after being refused reinforcements by the Confederate High Command, was ordered back to Virginia. Longstreet's Corps was to reinforce Lee against the advance of Meade and Grant for the spring campaign of 1864.

A young South Carolina soldier reflecting on his service during the Knoxville campaign called it, "the coldest and the wettest country I ever saw! It was no place to be without the proper food, clothes, blankets, or shoes, of which the soldiers had little."

...for shoes we were obligated to resort to the rawhides of beef cattle as temporary protection from the frozen ground. Then we began to find soldiers who could tan the hides of beeves, some who could make shoes, some who could make shoe pegs, some who could make shoe lasts, so it came about that the hides passed rapidly from the beeves to the feet of the soldiers in the form of comfortable shoes. Then [with] the opening of the railroad...[came] a shipment of three thousand shoes from General Lawton, Quartermaster-General.[9]

According to quartermaster correspondence, Longstreet also received a quantity of imported blankets as part of a shipment to the Army of Tennessee in mid-January, 1864. Ten thousand new uniforms were also requisitioned. In the interim, articles of clothing and homespun cloth from the, "hand-looms of the [local] farmers" helped to patch britches and jackets.[10]

"Those serving in Northern Virginia and the mountainous district should be preferred."

— Secretary of War J. Seddon, November 14, 1863.

The Army of Northern Virginia was compelled to halt active operations twice in the winter months of 1863 due to a shortage of warm clothing and shoes. First, during the Bristoe campaign of October 7–14, and again during the Mine Run campaign of November 26–27. Lee, in his own words, "was adverse to marching...at a season when frosts are certain and snows probable, unless [the men] were better provided."[1]

> **"East vs. West." Clothing for our Armies.**
>
> There is one subject which demands the immediate attention of the Government… it is the comfort of the Southern soldiers of the Army of Tennessee…. We venture the assertion that there is no other army in the Confederacy that has suffered more than this noble army in our front, which so many of our contemporaries delight to distinguish as, "Bragg's Army." The Army of Virginia, thanks to the occasional successful advance…supplies itself with clothing, flies, tents, boots, etc. in the enemy's country. Not so with the Army of the West. The boys of Bragg's Army have not had a grab since the Perryville campaign. Besides, alas, we are so far removed from Richmond. Unlike Lee's soldiers, those of Braggs do not come under the immediate supervision of the powers that be…. Our lines extend across the valley, which is drained by Chattanooga Creek, and as you may imagine, the condition of the men, especially those in the trenches and on picket is exceedingly uncomfortable. Not one of them have more than one blanket, and nearly all that belong to General Bragg's original army, are without shelter or any kind. Longstreet's Corps is somewhat better off. His men having provided themselves with Yankee flies, India rubbers, etc. at Chancellorsville and other battlefields.
>
> *Chattanooga Rebel*, October, 1863.
>
> Lee's Army was given preferential treatment by order of the Secretary of War on November 14, 1863.

On October 23, 1863, General Lee, in a letter to Secretary of War James A. Seddon, begged him to, "endeavor to provide the Army with shoes, clothing and blankets, for the season is approaching when the want of these articles will entail great suffering and sickness on the troops and incapacitate them for military movements."[2] And again on November 10, Lee urged Seddon's attention, "to the fact that many of the men in this Army are still barefooted and the weather has become cold."[3]

Four days later, Seddon replied that he had, "instructed the Quartermaster-General to send forward whatever small supplies he could command from the city [Richmond], or any other convenient Depots in the State."[4]

Many soldiers who served believed that Lee's Army of Northern Virginia was given preferential treatment over the other armies in the Confederacy. In a statement that confirms that belief, Seddon added, "I have directed that if our supplies are to be limited to allow due provision for all armies, those serving in Northern Virginia and the mountainous district [Shenandoah], "should be preferred!"[5]

The Army of Northern Virginia, given preferential treatment under orders from the Secretary of War, should have been the better off logistically of the two armies. Contemporary sources tell a different story, however, and such an order might have been appropriate under the circumstances. Letters from Dalton, Georgia, by April 1864, tell of an abundance of clothing, so much so that they were sending it away for storage. From Private Samuel Kitterick, 16th South Carolina Infantry:

> Dalton, Georgia
> April 27, 1864.
>
> Dear Wife,
>   We are expecting something to do here before long. We have received orders to move all surplus baggage to the rear. We have boxed our heavy and surplus baggage to be sent off for home. The box sent to Mr. Burditt you will find I have sent home a pair of shoes and my old pantaloons. I can draw plenty of clothing here and if we have to march I cannot carry it. I wish I had not brought so many [clothes] from home.[6]

Other soldiers writing from Dalton described the Army of Tennessee:

> [We are in] the finest trim. The men throughout are in the finest spirits that I ever saw and have no other idea that we will be in Middleton, Tennessee this spring…. I have about everything Ma that I need. I have uniforms enough to last me until next winter at least, but would like to have a few brown linen shirts. The greatest privation we have to endure now is doing without coffee.[7]

Private S. W. Holliday of the 55th Tennessee Infantry, writing from Camp Cummings, Mobile, Alabama, on April 1, 1864, also mentions, "We are stationed at this place and doing guard duty, but getting good rations and are very well clothed, and are much better than being on those heavy marches and retreats like the last one we were on in Mississippi under General Polk."[8]

While the soldiers of the Army of Tennessee fared well enough, General Robert E. Lee had to make some hard decisions to keep his men fed and equipped for service. The Impressment Law, a law Lee questioned as to its fairness and accountability, was forced on him during December 1863. Lee, in a letter to Colonel L.B. Northrop, Commissary General, C.S. Army, Richmond, wrote: "I regret to learn that the necessity for impressment by commanders of armies has, in your opinion, arrived. I shall endeavor to collect all the supplies for the army that I can legitimately do, and keep it in the best condition I can."[9]

Writing to General Early on December 22, Lee ordered Early to, "avail yourself...to collect and bring away everything that can be useful to the army from those regions that are open to the enemy." Besides food supplies like cattle, sheep, hogs and bacon, Lee wanted all the, "cloth and leather" Early could find.[10] To his quartermaster at Staunton, Virginia, Major H. M. Bell, Lee sent orders to provide, "transportation for all of Early's collected supplies." Lee also wanted Bell to, "send your agents with the army and wherever you can buy supplies belonging to your Department, particularly horses, horse shoes, cloth and leather, to do so."[11]

McHenry Howard, a Marylander, fought in the Army of Northern Virginia. In his memoirs, he described how Lee had ordered the creation of shoe shops to make and repair footwear:

> The shoemakers in the different regiments, seventeen I think, were encouraged to send home, and in some instances were given leave to go for their tools, and were put to work repairing shoes, being exempted from guard and other routine camp duty, but ready to fall in with their command on any call to arms. The shoe shops were in a separate camp of tents...from memory the saving was stated to have been certainly several hundred pairs, besides the men's feet were kept in better condition by the correction of ill fitting shoes.[12]

By mid-February, 1864, one Mississippi soldier commented:

> ...a pair of shoes...are less difficult to obtain now than in the past. In our Brigade we have a number of shoemakers, (3 in our regiment) who if they obtain tools and leather should be able to make 20 pairs of shoes a day.... Leather will be furnished by the Government. In the past, much of it came from saddle skirts, cartridge boxes, and other items which had been left unguarded. Some (the owners) called that stealing. Others called it using military equipment effectively.[13]

With the success of the shoe shops, Lee wanted to establish tailor shops to patch and mend clothing. His requests for finished leather and scraps of cloth and thread from the depot factories in Richmond went unanswered. All the plans Lee had for establishing his own army depot were suspended with the opening of the spring campaign in May 1864.

It is difficult at this time without all the inspection and quartermaster reports to state with any degree of accuracy how the Army of Virginia looked and was equipped for May, 1864. Those inspection reports available, though small in number, describe the clothing as, "Indifferent or Very Indifferent," meaning mixed and un-uniform, but adequate for the cold weather.[14]

One soldier remembered the winter of 1863-64, writing that, "clothing was not plentiful, nor blankets, nor shoes, and those that were issued were inferior. Large boxes of provisions were sent us by our friends at home...the Ladies Association in different parts of South Carolina forwarded considerable supplies of clothing at great trouble and still greater expense to themselves."[15]

Soldiers were still asking for donations, but the quantity sent had to be smaller than in previous years considering the shortages. Begging would be a more appropriate term to describe the entreaties of this 12th Louisiana soldier, cut off from home:

> Many of the soldiers are desperate of socks. Many more have not a single blanket, quilt, or coverlet of any kind to protect them from the chilling blasts of winter which has already lowered her heavy mantel around us, and the sad condition is representative of the brigade, Bufords, to which I belong. This Government no doubt has been doing all it could to meet this exigency, but as yet little has been done to alleviate the suffering.
>
> While thousands are given for the distribution of tracts and other religious literature, which without contradiction is a noble work, I think something can be done to alleviate the suffering of your noble soldiers. Come forward and clothe your soldiers, and they will defend your country.[16]

"In nearly all the branches of supply...we are not yet exempt from dependence on foreign importation."

— James A. Seddon,
November 26, 1863.

In a special report to Jefferson Davis, Secretary of War Seddon made the following statement:

> That they [The Quartermaster and Commissary Departments] have had during the last year [1863], extraordinary difficulties to encounter. The manufacturing operations of the [Quartermaster Department] have indeed been conducted on a grand scale, and have made more nearly the supplies for the Army from internal resources, but still for some essential articles such as shoes, blankets, and woolen cloth, partial dependence on importations could not be avoided.[1]

That the importations of war material helped to prolong the ability of the Confederacy to wage war there is no question. Millions of dollars worth of guns, powder, swords, accoutrements, cannon, machinery, medicines, chemicals, lead, food, shoes, cloth, clothing, and blankets, were purchased overseas to help sustain the armies as well as the civilian population.

It is beyond the scope of this book to give any kind of detailed history of the operations of the Confederate overseas trade, its financing, and blockade running in general. Besides the purchases made by the Confederate government, private contractors, state governments, and even Northern merchants dabbled in the lucrative business of shipping supplies to the South. Included are some of the actual numbers of goods reported by the Quartermaster Bureau. An exact accounting of all that was imported into the South is an unknown.

From February 1861 to February 1863, Major Caleb Huse, special purchasing agent in England for the Confederate States Government, had purchased and shipped out the following quartermas-

---

"Valuable Cargoes."

A conscript just from Wilmington, N.C. reports that within the past few days seventeen large steamers have arrived at that port, having run the blockade, loaded with stores for the Confederate Army. Among which are ninety-six thousand English rifles, one hundred and sixty thousand army blankets, one hundred and thirty-one thousand ready made uniforms, and thirty-six thousand pairs of army shoes, eleven locomotives, six rifled cannon, five cargoes of railroad iron, and skillful men accompanying them.

— *Savannah News*

This bit of information from a contemporary Southern paper is interesting, but doubtful. The arrival of 137,000 ready made uniforms for distribution to the Confederate army is mentioned nowhere else, in reports, records, or memoirs. One should be skeptical of newspaper reports.

Columbus (Georgia) Daily Enquirer, August 8, 1863

"How the Rebels Are Clothed."

The Wilmington, N.C. papers are full of advertisements offering for sale the cargo goods which have run the blockade. Sugar is selling for three cents a pound owing to the immense quantity on hand. All the railroads from Wilmington are at work day and night, to the exclusion of all other business, conveying supplies into the interior. Over 200 steamers and vessels belonging to different lines are engaged in running the blockade into this one point. Governor Vance says in his message that the State of North Carolina has received enough clothing through this channel to clothe her troops till January, 1865.

Fox Lake (Wisconsin) Gazette, December 30, 1863.

Governor Vance was very proud of his state's blockade running business, but unwilling to share a lot of it with his government.

ter items: 74,006 pairs of boots, 62,025 blankets, 78,520 yds. of cloth, 8,675 greatcoats, 8,250 pairs of trousers, 170,024 pairs of socks, 6,703 shirts, 17,894 yds. of flannel, 97 packages of trimmings, 34,731 sets of accoutrements, 40,240 gun slings, 37,655 knapsacks, 4,000 canteen straps, 81,406 bayonet scabbards, and 650 sets of sergeants' accoutrements. Another 13,750 pairs of trousers, 14,250 greatcoats, and 1,804 pairs of boots were waiting to be shipped from London as of December 15, 1862.[2]

From November 1, 1863, to December 15, 1864, through the blockade into Wilmington and Charleston came 669 packages or bales of leather, 545,000 pairs of boots and shoes, and 316,000 blankets.[3]

Besides blankets and shoes, in a period starting October 25 to December 6, 1864, another 62 bales of shirts, 20 bales of socks, 48 bales of cloth, 47 bales of flannel, 9 cases of buttons, 7 bales of woolen cloth, and 2 cases of caps, reached the southern shore.[4]

The Confederate States of Virginia, Georgia, Alabama, Texas, South Carolina, and especially North Carolina, conducted their own blockade running ventures. Governor Vance of North Carolina called the blockading business done through his state one of the, "greatest achievements of his administration."[5]

Large quantities of machinery supplies, 60,000 pairs of handcards [needed for weaving raw wool into cloth]...leather and shoes to 250,000 pairs, 50,000 blankets, gray woolen cloth for at least 250,000 uniforms, 12,000 overcoats, 37,092 pairs of socks, 1,956 Angola shirts, and 7,872 gray flannel shirts, were imported by North Carolina.[6] Vance boasted, "the supplies of shoes, blankets, and clothing more than sufficient for the supply of the North Carolina troops."[7]

By the end of the late war period, it was said that the seaports of Wilmington and Charleston were as important strategically to the South as the city of Richmond, Virginia. Without their lifeline to Europe, the Army of Northern Virginia would starve, and its soldiers would go naked and shoeless.

That line was severed on January 15, 1865. After a tremendous naval bombardment by over 50 vessels and an amphibious landing, Fort Fisher, Wilmington's main defensive work, fell to the enemy. The blockade runners for a time switched their operations to Charleston, South Carolina, but that city fell soon after on February 18, 1865.

The end of the War was only months away.

Confederate Cavalry Prisoners, Fairfax Court House, June, 1863.

This famous photograph of Confederate cavalryman captured at the Battle of Aldie, Virginia, June 17, 1863, depicts so well the phrase, "no two dressed alike," "half civilian, half military," we see over and over again in this book. Regular Confederate Cavalryman in short jackets, frock coats, some in civilian clothing, some wearing caps, most in light colored bee-hives, and linen or cotton overalls is hard on the eyes. I wonder, if this group came to a modern day reenactment, would half of them be told they must camp with the civilians?

CHAPTER 3
Late War Period, November 1864 – April 1865

"The demand for shoes will soon be greater than ever."

— Q.M. Gen'l. Lawton,
April 13, 1864.

Quartermaster Lawton and his department had again suffered through another winter of complaints, shortages, and a barrage of official correspondence. Despite the tremendous output of depots set up all over the South, the winter of 1863-64 was a rough one for the soldiers of the Confederacy. Their only salvation was the timely arrival of blockade goods, shoes, and blankets, enough to keep the armies one step ahead of actual deprivation. For Lawton, it meant redoubling his efforts to increase the amount of stores produced and imported for the Quartermaster Department. The coming spring campaign of 1864 and the following summer would again use up all QM supplies.

New laws by the Confederate Congress mandated a set percentage of cargo space for government cotton, and limited imports to only those items essential to the war effort (no more brandy or ladies' hoops). This placed the different Bureaus in a favorable position with foreign suppliers. The new cotton priorities helped to strengthen Confederate credit overseas.

In March 1864, Lawton placed an order for machinery to manufacture shoes and blankets. Lawton ordered the quartermaster in Nassau, Major R. P. Waller, to advance his agent, Mr. Thomas Sharp, the funds necessary to complete the purchase. Lawton stressed the importance of getting his machinery, stating that, "in a couple of months the department will be able to command quite a considerable quantity of leather." He added, "The facilities will enable this Department in a great measure independent of detailed labor." He felt that the machinery was a better investment than the outright purchase of ready-made shoes and blankets. From his correspondence, it is clear that he was trying to strengthen the domestic market at home, wanting to rely less on the blockaders and the uncertainty that went with overseas trading. Lawton could never forget the capture of the steamers Hebe and Venus in the fall of 1863. The trouble it caused his department for the next six months in trying to make up the loss he did not want to suffer through again.[1]

The following April, 1864, he ordered the suspension of blanket purchases for the Army altogether, but wanted shoes and especially wool cloth, "a good article of each," to be sent out. The scarcity of raw wool, "in this region of the country compels me [Lawton] to look abroad for material for clothing."[2]

With a wool shortage, the depots began to produce clothing made of cotton, the one material the South had in abundance. The only complaint heard from the soldiers was that cotton uniforms were issued in the dead of winter, and the cotton jackets and pants were too thin to keep the men warm.

The Quartermaster Department also entered into private contracts overseas with certain individuals for full uniforms ready-made. Mr. James L. Tait of Ireland made a deal to supply 50,000 overcoats and complete suits, flannel shirts, and 100,000 pairs of shoes, socks, and blankets. All was to be shipped within three months starting January 1, 1864.[3]

A number of Tait contract jackets have survived in museums and private collections. From references, it is known that Tait clothing was issued to those troops serving in the Petersburg - Appomatax campaigns, Army of Northern Virginia, and to a much lesser extent, in North Carolina in late 1864-early 1865, to those forces serving under General Joseph E. Johnston.[4]

On the home front, Lawton faced the most difficult task of trying to renegotiate with certain

Southern states the exclusive control of all their factory mills, pricing, and output share for his department. An appeal by the governor of Virginia in July 1864 for state control of one of Virginia's largest mills, the Matoaca Manufacturing Company of Petersburg, for the benefit of soldier families, brought a sharp response from Quartermaster Lawton. Lawton, although in sympathy with the hardships suffered by the civilian population, felt, "that it would be better for the State authorities to allow this department to control [all] the factory products, so far as they may be needed for military purposes.... The necessities of the people and objects of charity must be postponed until the wants of the Army [are satisfied]."[5]

Lawton had a personal ax to grind against Governor Vance of North Carolina, who had recently accused Lawton of, "scheming against [his state]" through the conscription laws.[6] Vance said Lawton was closing down factories in North Carolina if they didn't submit to Quartermaster Department control, with Vance threatening that, "it would not be submitted [by me]!" Lawton defended himself by stating that he had no control over the Conscription Bureau, or the Bureau of Foreign Supply, nor had he made any suggestions to either Bureau to interfere with North Carolina's quartermaster operations or blockade running for the benefit of the government.

Lawton also made it very clear to the Secretary of War that North Carolina had no agreement with the Confederate Government that he could find on record where, "the resources of North Carolina were dedicated to exclusive benefit of the troops there from." Lawton stated that twice a negotiation was attempted with North Carolina to try to gain some control over its output of clothing and material. Both times it was rejected and while soldiers of other states suffered for clothing, North Carolina had a year's reserve on hand and in storage.[7]

The only concession made by Governor Vance in three years was the issuance of 10,000 suits of clothing to the Army of Tennessee in 1864, 14,000 to Longstreet's Corps, Spring 1864, and another 10,000 turned over to the quartermaster for general issue in July-August 1864.[8] Lawton referred to the situation with North Carolina as an injustice, and further stated that his department had been issuing clothing to needy North Carolina troops all along. Vance owed him, and not the other way around!

War Governor of North Carolina Zebulon B. Vance, shown in this print, (far right) as Colonel of the 26th North Carolina Infantry.

Zebulon B. Vance, 1830-1894, officer, governor, and U.S. senator. As wartime governor, he firmly believed in states' rights over government impressment policies out of Richmond. He and Quartermaster General Lawton disagreed on issues of commutation monies for uniforms, blockade running, manufacturing facilities in North Carolina, and draft exemptions for North Carolina workers. Vance won, and became one of North Carolina's favorite sons.   Author's collection

The War would end before anything was resolved concerning who would control the factories in North Carolina or any other Confederate state. States' rights had won out, the Confederate Government itself not wanting a confrontation. A spirit of cooperation and fairness was the goal, sometimes at a greater cost than the government could bear.

Lawton did seem pleased with the way the quartermaster operations were running and felt prepared for the coming winter of 1864-65. In September 1864, in a letter to a Major J. B. Fraser in London, Lawton wished him to purchase material for officer's uniforms, stationary, and leather. Lawton also ordered Fraser, "not to contract for blue cloth for pants, as gray makes up to more advantage." Lawton requested more woolen cloth or flannels, a cheap and serviceable hat for the Army, the best blankets, and gray cloth with a fair, "proportion of trimmings" for the winter season. There seemed no urgency in Lawton's correspondence as in the previous winter of 1863-64.[9]

Lawton capped off the last two quarters of 1864 with a Quartermaster's Report to a Special Congressional Committee in Richmond. Despite the supply complaints heard again from the Army of Northern Virginia, Lawton explained that the department goals had been met and that the, "armies have been fully supplied."

On February 10, 1865, the Quartermaster-General submitted a special report to a select committee of the Confederate Congress. Contained in this report were the actual field issues of clothing for the fourth quarters of 1864 through February 1865 to the armies of the Confederate States. The reasons for the investigation into quartermaster operations were a series of complaints and eyewitness testimony by both officers and men of not enough clothing and shoes being issued. It was rags and bare-feet again for a good part of 1864-1865.

Lawton, in defense of his Department, claimed, "considering Departmental goals of providing a suit of clothing every six months for each man in service. [and the amount of clothing actually issued], any complaints of shortages were due to an imperfect distribution of supplies and waste on the part of the individual soldiers, or both."[10]

Under the Act of Congress approved on October 8, 1862, and the regulations of the Confederate States Army, the clothing required in the third year of service would be: one cap and cover, one jacket, two pairs of pants, three shirts, two pairs of drawers, four pairs of shoes, four pairs of socks, and one blanket.

In checking the numbers of articles issued against the number of men present in the field, Lawton remarked, "that the issues of shirts, shoes, drawers, and caps may in some instances appear light, as large stocks had been distributed earlier." Commenting further, Lawton states, "with the exception of overcoats and the item of flannel undershirts . . . the armies have been fully supplied."[11]

If the numbers stated in Lawton's report were accurate, Lawton was correct. In fact, the special investigating committee exonerated Lawton and his department for any blame as to the conditions of the army. They found that any shortages were due primarily to, "soldiers improvidence." Also discovered by the committee was that large quantities of soldiers clothing were ending up in the civilian market. "A walk through the business streets in Richmond will satisfy anyone to this fact!," quipped the committee chairman. Lawton himself was aware of the sale or barter of government clothing and felt strongly that it should be stopped.[12]

Besides the soldiers, the subordinate quartermaster officers took part or much of the blame by the committee for the state of affairs. A suggestion was strongly urged by the committee that the regimental officers direct more of their attention to the so-called battlefield losses of clothing with a goal of, "lessening them by a more careful observation."[13]

1862 photo of Zeb Vance.

This photo illustrates the commonly-held perception of Zeb Vance as Governor of the State of North Carolina. You would not want to meet Vance in a dark alley somewhere in Raleigh.   North Carolina Archives

House of Representatives, Feb. 11, 1865. Resolutions adopted, and report ordered to be printed.

Report

Of Special Committee on the Pay and Clothing of the Army.

In regards to the clothing furnished the soldiers and non-commissioned officers, the committee especially refer to the letters of the Quartermaster General of December 12th, 1864, and January 27th, 1865, and the statement referred to in.... It appears there has been issued to the armies in the field, during the last six months, to December 31st, and including to 21st January 1865, to Lee's Army the following articles of clothing:

Jackets	215,592
Pants	356,729
Shoes, Pairs	359,937
Blankets	131,477
Hats and Caps	116,637
Flannel Shirts	22,503
Cotton Shirts	285,944
Drawers	341,682
Socks	271,285
Overcoats	6,655

Of this quantity, the State of North Carolina furnished her soldiers as follows:

Jackets	21,301
Pants	32,104
Shoes	9,263
Blankets	1,696
Hats and Caps	12,751
Cotton Shirts	23,354
Drawers	22,519
Socks	15,059
Overcoats	200

No other States are included in the above numbers, although Georgia has issued during the past year the following amounts:

Jackets	26,745
Pants	28,808
Shoes, Pairs	37,657
Blankets	7,504
Shirts	24,952
Drawers	24,168
Socks	23,024

In this report, Quartermaster General Lawton was absolved from any blame for shortages of clothing and shoes in the Confederate Army. Soldiers' improvidence in taking care of their clothing, trading with civilians, speculators, and incompetent regimental quartermaster officers were the reasons their Congress believed they were short of clothing.

A second charge leveled by the Congressman was that certain officers showed "[little] energy or promptness or care in their duties, whose business it is to distribute clothing in the field." The quartermaster officers denied these charges, and demanded an investigation into the persons or papers giving the evidence.[14]

While some of the privates were indeed guilty in the illicit trade of C. S. clothing, or lied to their officers about how they lost their greatcoat and blanket in the last skirmish, the shortages in clothing were all too real. Mostly, the shortages were the result of battlefield conditions and logistics, including a lack of soap and water to wash clothes, firewood to boil the water, and no pay for months that left many in threadbare uniforms.

The long, hard campaigning of the summer, fall, and winter of 1864-65 had stretched the South's transportation facilities to the limit. The depots had the clothes; the men just wore them out too fast in the field, and they were difficult to replace when the armies were on the move.

"Clothing was sparsely issued.... Shoes were scarce. I do not remember the issue of a single overcoat, and but a few blankets."

— J. Caldwell, 1st S.C. Inf.

The opening campaigns of Spring 1864, Atlanta in the West, and the Wilderness in the East, would be followed by a summer of continuous fighting on both fronts. The two largest armies, Lee's and Johnston's, were said to be in high spirits and in good condition, but heavily outnumbered. The only shortages reported, and of great concern to both commanders, was that of wagon transportation and horses to pull them.

When the battles for Atlanta began in early May 1864, the number of wagons assigned to each brigade, as one officer put it, "were reduced to the lowest limit," only 18 wagons, seven ambulances, and one forage for 2,000 men and officers, six wagons for officer's baggage, five for ammunition, one for ordnance, four for cooking utensils and rations, one for animal forage, and one for medical supplies for the brigade. No listing is given for quartermaster clothing, and from references, it is evident that clothing stocks were stuck into any available space.[1] An interesting story comes out of the Texas Brigade, Army of Northern Virginia, to help illustrate this point:

> Headquarters, 5th Texas Regt.
> July 15, 1864
>
> This is to certify that on the 25th day of April, 1864, I was ordered by the Lt. Colonel K. Bryan, Comd. 5th Texas Infantry, to receive from Major J. H. Littlfield Q. M., the following invoice of clothing and to issue the same, which I did, Viz.: 250 pairs of pants, 100 jackets, 225 shirts, 225 drawers, and 22 pairs of shoes.
>
> After the Regt. was supplied we were ordered to march immediately for the Wilderness, the remainder of the boots were put in the staff wagon, and after Captain Norwood returned, the goods were found to be short as follows viz: 17 pairs of pants, 8 jackets, 25 shirts, 27 pairs of drawers, 6 pairs of shoes.
>
> It was impossible to furnish a guard for the clothing, all the men were needed in the ranks and no blame can be attached to Captain Norwood, he being absent on duty.
>
> B. P. Fuller,
> 1st Lt., Co. A, 5th Texas.[2]

Besides the 5th Texas, all of Longstreet's Corps was re-uniformed in April 1864, a gift from the State of North Carolina. One Ohio lieutenant wrote immediately following the Battle of the Wilderness how he:

> ...had the pleasure of seeing about 4,000 prisoners passing on their way to the rear. They seemed completely surprised, which is a wonder for old troops. As to their appearance, they were all clad in neat gray jackets and pantaloons with entire seats. In contrast we [the Yankees] were in rags. Scarcely one of us having a complete garment of any sort.[3]

After the bloody stalemate at the Wilderness came Spotsylvania Courthouse, the North Anna battles, horrific Cold Harbor, the early fighting around Petersburg, and the following siege of that city. One Confederate officer called it an, "eleven months battle," starting May 5, 1864, to the surrender in April, 1865, at Appomattox. Union General Grant would continue his war of attrition, stretching Lee's lines around Petersburg to the limit.

Tait Jackets, "Good News for Alabama Soldiers."

Four months ago a contract was entered into between the State of Alabama on the part of the Quartermaster General and the firm of Peter Tait & Co. Limerick, Ireland, through Major J. L. Tait, of the British army for a large quantity of military clothing for the Alabama soldiers. Quartermaster Green stipulated that a large portion of the goods to be furnished initially cut (kits), with the necessary trimmings-affording employment to the seamstresses and tailors of our home factories. Some thousands of these uniforms we are glad to announce, have safely arrived in the Confederacy.... The outfit consists of a jacket, pants, shoes, and overcoat of the most substantial material – the cloth being exactly that used in the British army....

Some of the goods for our State troops is already made up into uniforms.... Several thousand of these uniforms are already here. The rest of the order will be here in a few days.

Alabama did indeed contract and receive uniforms from the Peter Tait & Co. of Limerick, Ireland. What is more interesting is that Major Tait himself traveled the South, signing contracts all over the Confederacy for clothing.

Columbus (Georgia) Daily Enquirer, October 22, 1864

Tait Jackets for North Carolina?

Did North Carolina have a contract to purchase Tait jackets from overseas? The following extract from the North Carolina Quartermaster Department, Raleigh, November 17, 1864, poses the question:

The operations of the Quartermaster Department of this State for the six months ending September 30, 1864, have been chiefly confined to the purchase of material and the manufacturing of clothing for our troops and the supply of the Home Guards when in active service and the State Troops.

A portion of the clothing for our troops has been purchased from our own factories...*A large portion has been brought in from foreign countries.*

For March 3, 1865, 110 jackets; March 4, 1865, 50 jackets; March 6, 1865, 20 jackets.

See also, Fred P. Todd Collection Notes, North Carolina. Brown University Special Collections; Jensen, Leslie D., *Johnny Reb, The Uniform of the Confederate Army, 1801-1865*.

A North Carolina Tait jacket?

This illustration is taken from a photo of a jacket in the collection of the Greensboro Historical Museum, Greensboro, North Carolina. The jacket belonged to a Private Gauge of the 58th North Carolina Infantry. The 58th ended its service with the Confederacy guarding quartermaster supplies in Greensboro in April 1865. Is this a North Carolina Tait imported jacket or issued from some other depot? The jacket is made from a fine grade blue-gray English cloth, the collar and shoulder tabs piped in light blue.

See also, Jensen, Leslie D., "A Survey of Confederate Quartermaster issue Jackets, Part 2.," *Military Collector and Historian Journal*, Spring, 1990.

PART THREE

"The Army pay is in arrears for several months. This is an excuse for desertion, the sale of clothing, equipments and ammunitions by the soldiers."

— John C. Breckinridge,
C. S. Secretary of War.

Uniform descriptions for the Late War Period are few in number, but what we do have is the actual field issues of clothing distributed by the C.S. Quartermaster Department from July 1864 to January 1865.

The Army of Northern Virginia was well supplied. A total of 104,199 jackets, 140,578 pants, 167,862 pairs of shoes, 74,851 blankets, 27,011 hats and caps, 21,068 flannel shirts, 157,727 cotton shirts, 170,139 cotton drawers, 146,136 pairs of socks, and 4,861 overcoats were requisitioned and issued through Richmond. The only items in short supply were overcoats, socks, and flannel shirts. Taking the average strength of the A.N.V. at 55,000 - 77,000 men, plus or minus, that would give each man approximately 2 jackets, 3 pairs of pants, 3 pairs of shoes, 1 blanket, 3 pairs of socks, maybe a hat or cap, flannel shirt and overcoat if lucky, and at least 3 sets of underwear for a period of eight months.

This amount of clothing seems more than sufficient, and was a greater issue quantity than called for in the regulations. These figures are important as they show the Army of Northern Virginia was not as ragged and barefoot in the closing months of the Civil War as is commonly believed.

What has come down to the reader of today is what is called "popular history." A story is repeated so often as to replace the truth of what really happened. Most people believe the tattered, ragged, shoeless, and starving Rebel soldier description came out of the late war period only and was responsible in good part for the Confederate surrender. This picture has made it easier for us and them at that time to accept Appomattox. People eulogized the old Confederate veterans who, it was said, suffered tremendously under great personal privation against a numerically superior and better equipped Federal force. But, if bare-feet and rags were the only reason for losing the War, then the Confederates should have surrendered in the fall of 1862!

The saga and tradition of the ragged Rebel fighting to the bitter end is real 19th century romanticism in its finest form, and forsaking some historical facts, is only partially true. What really defeated the Southern armies and particularly Robert E. Lee's forces were not just bullets and shells and a lot of Yankees, but something just as dangerous to Lee's forces, the financial collapse of the Confederate currency. By 1864, $70 in Confederate paper was worth only $1 in coin.[1]

A case in point was the report of Major A. H. Cole, Inspector General, Field Transportation, C. S. Army. Major Cole had been asked to comment on the ability of the Quartermaster Department to supply enough horses and mules for the spring campaigns of 1865. Cole stated that 6,000 horses and mules were needed, and that only 500 animals were available east of the Mississippi by impressment. This left a shortage of 5,500. Cole stressed that such shortages would undoubtedly, "check military operations."[2]

Cole's only solution was to buy horses in Mexico, Virginia, or Mississippi, across enemy lines and for hard cash. "Gold or Federal money would work," stated Cole, or cotton, "600 pounds for first class artillery horses," 500 pounds second class, and 400 pounds for third class." Confederate money or bonds were no longer accepted, being too risky. Cole warned, "the officers must have the cotton or gold in hand" or the sales could not be completed.[3]

The Quartermaster Department also complained to Congress about the shortages of funds to keep the war going. It was reported that a debt of $5,000,000 was still owed for factory goods and services, "long since delivered." Without the money, the factories would be forced to sell their wares on the open market, and not to the Government.[4]

The Sustenance Bureau claimed in March 1865 that a sufficient surplus of food remained in Confederate hands in Virginia, North Carolina, upper South Carolina, and East Tennessee, enough to feed the Army for four months. An immediate supply of funds, $70,000,000 was requested at once, "in gold or U. S. paper currency," not Confederate bonds or bank notes. Without the hard cash the system, it was said, "would be paralyzed."[5]

Even if the gold or Federal dollars could be raised, the army unfortunately had to be supplied

Ragged Rebels?

Private James English and friend, 21st Virginia Infantry, June 12, 1864.

This great photograph helps depict the "Ragged Rebel" of the late war period we read so much about in Civil War history. Quartermaster records show that over 356,000 pairs of trousers were issued to Lee's army in the last quarter of 1864. Why this soldier is wearing a pair of trousers with the knees out, with all the clothing available, is unknown. Perhaps he was overdrawn on clothing, or he traded his new trousers for a chicken, or the next day he was issued a new pair of trousers. Each Confederate regiment and soldier had his own story to tell on how they kept themselves clothed during the war.

USMHI

Two Union Officers who escaped from Confederate prison in North Carolina and reached the Union lines at Loudon, Tennessee, on January 2, 1865.

In order to escape, these two Union officers from Wisconsin assumed the guise of Confederate soldiers. They would have fooled anyone they encountered other than a Confederate patrol. The man on the right wears what appears to be a Columbus Depot style jacket. Although Federals, these two would fit right in with the 21st Virginia, ragged trousers and all.

USMHI

from a great distance. One hundred and twenty tons of commissary supplies would have to be moved daily over a rail system described as, "the least able to bear it."[6]

The Superintendent of Railroads, Lieutenant-Colonel F. W. Sims, referred to the lines that served the Army of Northern Virginia around Petersburg as "overworked and not well attended." A shortage of good mechanics, iron rails, and steam engines, plagued the railroads and some serious talk was given to importing all three items to keep the roads running.[7]

A point of concern stressed by Sims was that considering the importance of the railroads to the armies' "comfort and safety, why were they offered so little protection?" Quartermaster Lawton also wanted protection for the rail lines. "The ability of this Bureau to supply the [armies] depends on their relative positions, and the preservation or destruction of our lines of transportation," he said.[8]

Secretary of War John C. Breckinridge was made painfully aware of the currency crisis and debt load being carried by the Confederacy, an estimated $200,000,000! Breckinridge condemned the disastrous effect it was having on the war effort and country:

The Army pay is in arrears for several months. This is an excuse for desertion, the sale of clothing, equipments, and munitions by the soldiers. Throughout the whole country discontent and discredit has arisen from the failure to pay for supplies of food and animals that have been impressed. It is plainly impossible to carry on any [War Department] operations under such a condition of things.[9]

❖ Late War Period, November 1864 – April 1865 ❖

An attempt was made by the Confederate government to raise $3,000,000 in silver, gold coin, or gold dust, to purchase food in Virginia. The loyal ladies gave up their jewelry for the soldiers, but it came too late, on March 17, 1865, to change the outcome of the War.[10]

Richard D. Goff, in his work, *Confederate Supply*, gives an overview of the condition of the Confederacy and its demise in the War's last days:

> [In 1864-1865] the Confederate forces were outmaneuvered and worn down until they delivered the railroad network and seaports to the enemy, bringing the war effort to a halt. In the final months of the struggle the dissolving armies wandered around the country, while the factories produced and the storehouses held supplies that could not be moved to the troops. Shortages had hamstrung the soldiers; the armies had failed to protect the supply efforts.[11]

In his memoirs, General E. P. Alexander, Lee's artillery commander, told of a secret report that came out just weeks before the surrender. It stated that there was not enough meat in the Confederacy to sustain its armies, that meat had to be imported from abroad, and it was; that the transportation system was not now adequate to meet the demands of the service; that clothing for the troops had to be moved by rail; and that the rail service here could only continue its operations if machine parts and rails could be purchased overseas.

When the ports of Wilmington and Charleston fell, the war was nearly over. In General Alexander's words, "every part had done its duty and lasted its time, and now everything was ready to go smash all at once!"[12] And smash it did for the Confederacy.

"We turned and scorched the seams of our underwear on account of insects, we had no way of boiling our clothing."

Confederate soldier, in the trenches at Atlanta.

On the same day that Grant advanced into the Wilderness in Virginia, May 5, 1864, Union General William T. Sherman began the campaign to take the important manufacturing city of Atlanta, Georgia. From the opening skirmishes near Tunnel Hill to the occupation of Atlanta on September 2, 1864, that long, hot summer saw almost continuous combat with little chance of rest or re-supply for either side.

Confederate General Joseph E. Johnston's Army of Tennessee, for the spring of 1864, was said to be reasonably well-equipped, clothed, and shod. It took seven weeks of battle and marching for a Texas soldier in June 1864 to sum up the condition of Johnston's command. He wrote eloquently that, "In this army, one hole in the seat of the breeches indicates a Captain, two holes a Lieutenant, and the seat of the pants all out indicates the individual is a private."[1]

Besides going ragged, there was little chance to wash what was worn. With most of the fighting done from trenches or behind log and dirt barricades, and the shortage of water, one C.S. officer lamented, "the task of keeping clean was to say the least a hard one."

Quartermaster records show that some clothing and shoes were distributed at Dalton, Georgia, and again at Atlanta during the siege from depot stocks. Actual numbers of issue were 45,412 jackets, 102,864 pants, 109,558 pairs of shoes, 27,000 blankets, 45,864 hats or caps, 61,860 cotton shirts, 108,937 pairs of drawers, and 55,560 pairs of socks, delivered from July 1864 to January 1865.[2]

Each man in Johnston's army, later Hood's army, for the summer and winter of 1864-65 would receive but one jacket (maybe), two pairs of pants, two or three pairs of shoes, maybe one blanket, if lucky, one hat or cap, one or two cotton shirts, two pairs of drawers, and one or two pairs of socks for five months of hard service.

Applying the formula that a uniform would last only three or four months in the field leaves a greater part of the Army of Tennessee in a ragged state and needing shoes. An August 18 report from the artillery arm of the service confirms this. A shortage of 1,935 coats, 1,974 blankets, 1,651 pairs of shoes, 4,564 pairs of socks, 1,710 haversacks, and 1,288 canteens for approximately 3,400 men was recorded. The Inspector General also found that when uniforms were issued to the artillery, blue-faced infantry uniforms were given instead of the proper red-faced for artillery. What frustrated him even more was that he claimed he saw, "jackets with the artillery trimmings in the infantry!"[3]

Hood's army as it passed, October 1864.

The following newspaper article described for the *Cincinnati Commercial* the appearance of the Confederate Army of Tennessee as it passed through Dalton, Georgia, in October 1864.

> They were ragged and thinly clad, having as a general thing only pantaloons, shirt and hat in their inventory of clothing; the first, greasy and tattered, the last shocking affairs in multitudinous variety.
>
> As a general thing they were tolerably well shod, though in one of Stewart's Divisions, one of our officers counted over three hundred barefooted privates....
>
> Not more than one in ten have blankets.... In the line, the distinction as to apparel between the officers and men was entirely obliterated!

The Army of Tennessee would receive needed clothing supplies in the following weeks, but only enough to supply the most needy. By necessity they were forced to use the captured overcoats, shoes, hats, and blankets of the Federal Army. Reprinted in the *Richmond Examiner*, November 7, 1864.

Lee White, Chicamauga Battlefield Park

**Longstreet's Moccasins,
"They were better than nothing."**

Private W. R. Houghton, Co. H., 15th Alabama Infantry, in his memoirs explained how to make a set of rawhide moccasins to cover your bare feet or when your soles wore out.

> "Sometimes an order would come for the barefoot to go to the butchers pen. A man would put his foot on the hairy side of a fresh cowhide and piece, heart shaped would be cut out. The holes were cut near the edges, and it was sewed with thongs of the same material over his feet. They were better than nothing for a time, but when wet by the rain, they became too large."

The use of rawhide moccasins is mentioned by General Longstreet during his Knoxville Campaign, and again by General Hood in the Franklin-Nashville Campaign.

Houghton, W.R., Houghton, W.B.
Two Boys in the Civil War and After,
Montgomery, AL: Paragon Press, 1912.

On July 17, 1864, General Joseph E. Johnston was relieved of command of the Army of Tennessee, having failed to arrest the advance of General Sherman into Georgia. General John Bell Hood of A.N.V. fame replaced Johnston as the new commander. Hood quickly developed plans to drive Sherman from Atlanta with a series of frontal assaults on the Union positions surrounding the city. The results were horrific. Over 12,500 casualties were recorded in a series of battles running from July 21–23. The Army of Tennessee was bloodied, almost broken.

General Hood, under siege and facing the possibility of being surrounded, ordered the evacuation of the city on September 2. One of the South's irreplaceable industrial centers had fallen to the Federal Army.

By some incredible blunder, the entire Confederate reserve supply of ammunition, over twenty-eight carloads, was left behind and ordered destroyed. The resulting explosions were heard for miles. Atlanta went out with a bang.

Besides ammunition, large quantities of food, quartermaster stores, and machinery, were lost to the mobs or burned. The Atlanta Cannon Foundry, the Western and Atlanta roundhouse and railroad yard with its equipment and rolling stock, the Confederate Arsenal and Rolling Mill, the Atlanta Machine Works, the Novelty Iron Works, and the Atlanta Quartermaster Depot and factory were gone. The loss of men in the defense of the city, an estimated 45,000 to 50,000, attributed to death, wounds, disease, and desertion was a tremendous blow to the Confederate war machine, and could not be replaced.

General Hood, his depleted Army now encamped at Palmetto Station, still believed he could save Atlanta. His new strategy was to get Sherman to leave the trenches around the city and bring him to battle. He would strike at Sherman's rear, severing the railroad north of Atlanta and Sherman's supply line to Nashville. The only thing Hood accomplished in all this was the destruction of the Army of Tennessee in his Nashville campaign. Hood's hope was that his movements north of Atlanta on September 29, 1864, would focus all of Sherman's attention on him, and not the Southern coastal cities as feared by the powers in Richmond.

Before the campaign started, Hood's army had to be re-outfitted. Requisitions were made for uniforms and shoes, and the orders were to be filled out of depot stocks in Columbus, Georgia, Columbus, Mississippi, and Demopolis, Alabama. It would be three weeks, though, before the quartermaster goods would reach Hood's army. To make do, the Confederates used the captured uniforms and food of their enemies, picked up along the way.

On October 2, three divisions of Stewart's Corps were ordered to destroy the Atlanta and Western railroad north of Marietta. Federal garrisons at Ackworth, Moon's Station, and Big Shanty, were by force of numbers, overwhelmed and captured by these troops. Walthall's Division of Alabama, Mississippi, and Arkansas soldiers captured the Union blockhouse at Moon's Station. One of the Federal prisoners, Aaron Smith, was a private in the 14th Illinois Infantry. Private Smith left an interesting account of the behavior and appearance of the Confederates after he was made a prisoner of war:

> As we marched out of the stockade...we found ourselves...surrounded by a howling mob of Confederates who unceremoniously relieved us of our watches, etc., and made all kinds of one-sided trades for our clothing, hats, boots, and shoes.
>
> At the time the Johnnies were robbing our effects they found me rather poorly clad. My pantaloons and blouse were quite threadbare, being considerably soiled, but I had on a good black hat which seemed attractive to them.... A Johnnie jerked it from my head and handed me his old quilted one. I had no sooner got this old quilted rag placed on my head when another Johnnie jerked mine off and handed me his own broken down broken-billed gray cap...and before I had gone another ten steps, another Johnnie [snatched] off my cap and handed me his hat! When I examined the old black and blue limp thing he handed me, I found the crown was an old piece of blue army overcoat which had "whanged on" with cotton cord, and the limp black rim was looped up to this on all sides with the same kind of cord.[4]

Private Smith was marched to Big Shanty and from there watched Hood's army as it passed on the way north to Dalton:

> [The] Confederate troops [were] principally infantry and artillery, with long trains of ambulances and provision wagons of every conceivable shape from light spring to old farm wagons, [and an] occasional good U. S. Army wagon. The mules and horses were as poor and motley looking as the vehicles. The most of them had on chain harnesses, cotton cloth back-bands, and corn-husk collars. The troops were poorly clad in brown and gray cotton suits, and but for the flags they carried, they might have been a section of the old Continental Army.[5]

A final comment from Private Smith on Hood's command was that they were in "good spirits," but from their general appearance, "we took considerable comfort in believing the Confederacy was on its last pegs."[6]

Continuing their march north, Hood's soldiers were repulsed at Altoona in one of the hottest little engagements of the War. They did succeed in taking Dalton, Georgia, on October 13, 1864. In the Union garrison was a regiment of black soldiers who were, "quickly divested of blankets, overcoats, shoes, and hats, and in many cases, their breeches."[7]

The Wilmington Daily Journal was quoted as saying that along with the Union prisoners, "a large quantity of shoes were captured." It was believed to be, "enough to supply the whole army!"[8]

Some shoes might have been taken, but the paper was wrong. When Hood's men finally reached Gladsen, Alabama, on October 20, not all could be supplied. Colonel Elliston Capers of the 24th South Carolina Infantry, noted in his campaign report that of the clothing received at Gladsen, 21 blankets, 112 pairs of pants, 74 pairs of shoes, 44 jackets, 82 pairs of socks, 37 shirts, and 46 pairs of drawers were not enough to supply all of his 285 men but relieved the most needy.[9]

More clothing and shoes followed and were distributed at Tuscumbia and Florence, Alabama, on October 31, and November 2, but again the issues were described as "inadequate." Hood himself complained that, "many of his men were again shoeless, or nearly so." An artilleryman in Guibor's Battery, while encamped at Tuscumbia, described his fellow soldiers as, "having a rather ragged, dilapidated appearance, and many were barefooted."[10]

Like Longstreet's men the winter before in East Tennessee, Hood's soldiers fashioned what they called "moccasins" out of rawhide in place of shoes. To add to their misery, a chilly rain came and it continued for ten straight days, turning the roads into a deep slippery mud. "The boys who wore moccasins had a deal of trouble when they got wet until they could dry them by the fire," recalled one soldier.[11] The rain continued as Hood's army entered Florence, Alabama.

The forward elements of the army finally met up with the Federals at Columbia, Tennessee. The Yankees were said to be entrenched and ready for a fight. Hood chose to bypass the Union command under General Schofield at Columbia, and race him to Nashville. Schofield realized his position was tenuous with Hood in his rear, and ordered a retreat to the Duck River. Schofield was flanked out of this position and continued his march north. Contact was made between the two forces at Spring Hill, Tennessee. Hood, surrounding Spring Hill, now believed he had Schofield trapped and at his mercy. Miraculously, Schofield managed to escape by marching quietly that night right through the Confederate camps that lined the road.

Hood was furious that Schofield had eluded him. He followed the Yankees to Franklin, Tennessee, where the Federals had dug in south of the small town. A frontal assault was ordered by Hood and the bloody Battle of Franklin commenced at 4:00 p.m. on November 30, 1864. Hood put 19,000 - 20,000 infantrymen into line. Advancing over open ground, they took the first line of Federal works, then charged at the double quick screaming the rebel yell. The Johnnies flung themselves on the second line of entrenchments that fronted the Carter house. It was slaughter. Hood lost from 6,000 to 8,000 men dead, wounded, and missing in five hours of bloody combat, much of it hand to hand. Five Confederate generals were killed: Cleburne, Adams, Strahl, Granbury, and Gist, in the vortex that swept around the Carter house and cotton gin.

The 700 to 1,000 Confederate prisoners taken at Franklin were said to be, "a hard looking set, lean, ragged and hungry."[12] Private Wideon Houghton, 23rd Michigan Infantry wrote that they, "looked as though they were starved...and they had no coats nor shoes not more than half of them, and they were all ragged and dirty, and they looked more like robbers than they did soldiers.... When they came in all they had in their haversacks was sugar cane and hickory nuts."[13]

Private Adam J. Weaver of the 104th Ohio made note of the Confederates' use of captured Union clothes. "The Rebel prisoners are nearly all wearing parts of our uniforms. This seems to be the common practice now. The Rebs rob our dead because they have nothing to wear, especially our shoes and [over]coats. They still retain their droopy felt hats which gives them a hayseedy look."[14]

Union General Schofield abandoned his positions around Franklin that night and made his escape by a forced march to Nashville. Hood followed him on the morning of December 1, 1864. What followed was pure folly on Hood's part. He laid siege to the city of Nashville on December 2, 1864. His tired and cold army was stretched thin around the Federal lines. On December 15 and 16, the Federals attacked in overwhelming numbers, breaking Hood's lines and turning the battle into a rout for some of the Confederates. Hood lost another 1,500 to 2,000 men killed and wounded, 54 cannon, and some 4,462 as prisoners.

The C. S. captives were rounded up, fed, and clothed by their enemies. It was a wonder to many of the Union men how these Southern soldiers fought as hard as they did. "They were bare-footed, bare-headed, half of them with only enough rags to cover their bodies. They threw down their arms and begged for something to eat. Every man that had an extra shirt or garment of any kind gave it to help cover their nakedness."[15]

The Confederate retreat from Nashville was cold, miserable, and painful, for Hood's barefooted soldiers. The worst cases were put aboard the wagons to save their feet. It was bloody footprints in the snow again for many of them. The army ended its retreat at Tupelo, Mississippi, on January 3, 1865. Only 17,709 infantry and artillery were reported as present, a difference of almost 23,000 men from the start of the campaign.

The soldiers took the time to rest and clean themselves up. An artilleryman in Lumsden's Battery, encamped at Iuka, Mississippi, detailed in his memoirs the appearance of the typical Confederate soldier of the Army of Tennessee at the end of the Nashville campaign:

> December, 1864.
>
> Recrossing the Tennessee River near Bainbridge, we camped a few days near Iuka, Miss., for rest and a general cleaning, but many soldiers had no clothing except the rags they had on.
>
> A Confederate private at the time consisted of a pair of old shoes or boots, soles gaping, and tied to the uppers with strings, no socks, threadbare pants, patched at the knees, burnt out at the bottom halfway to his knees, his calves black with smoke from standing with his back to the fire, his shirt sticking out of the holes in the rear of his pants, a weather beaten jeans jacket, out at the elbows and collar greasy, and an old slouch hat hanging about his face, with a tuft of hair sticking out of the crown. The officers did not show up much better.[16]

On January 10, a Confederate officer in Walthall's Division wrote how, "the army cannot muster 5,000 effect men [out of 17,000]. Many go home everyday never to return...nine-tenths of the line officers and men [left] are barefooted and naked."[17]

Three days later General Hood resigned and General Richard Taylor of the Department of Alabama was placed in command of the remnants of the Army of Tennessee. To improve morale, Taylor ordered clothing sent from his depots in Columbia, Tennessee, and from Mississippi and Alabama. The ragged artillerymen in Lumsden's Battery were issued, "new gray jackets and pants and linsey shirts, lately gotten from home [Alabama]" as part of Taylor's re-fit.[18]

Some of the 5th Tennessee soldiers of Strahl's Brigade were heartened when they arrived at their camp in Corinth, Mississippi, on January 2, 1865. Waiting for them was, "Lieutenant J. L. Lemonds with wagon loads of clothing etc., which he had collected for us in Henry County. As the boxes were opened many of us were made happy by the sight of warm clothing, so sorely needed."[19]

The remaining regiments were consolidated and ordered east to fight General Sherman in the Carolinas. Stephen D. Lee's Corps left on January 19, and Cheatham's Corps on the 20th. Stewart's Corps remained at Tupelo, but they too were eventually sent east to join Johnston's new army. General Joseph E. Johnston had recently been reinstated as commander of the remaining forces of the Army of Tennessee, as well as all the troops left in Georgia, Florida, and South Carolina.

On January 21, 1865, Cheatham's Corps was ordered to Bentonville, North Carolina, where Johnston had ordered a concentration of all of his available forces to contest Sherman's advance. A surprise attack was planned to fall on the forward moving Union 14th Corps.

In the two-day Battle of Bentonville, Johnston was forced to retreat after the Federals brought up some heavy reinforcements. Sherman followed Johnston until the word of General Lee's surrender was confirmed. Johnston asked for a meeting with Sherman to discuss an armistice. After some discussions on the terms proposed, Johnston formally surrendered on April 26, 1865, at the Bennet house near Durham, North Carolina. He had accepted the same conditions as General Lee. For the men of the Army of Tennessee, the War was over.

Confederate uniform descriptions at Johnston's surrender, unlike Lee's at Appomattox, are yet to be found. Contemporary reports peg Johnston's army as a band of ragged vandals. Governor Vance of North Carolina wanted compensation and protection for what he referred to as, "a lawless license of an army about to be disbanded." Confederate soldiers were taking clothing, shoes, blankets, and other stores from North Carolina warehouses by force. Vance had himself witnessed the sacking of a supply train at McLean's Station. "The roadsides and woods were crowded with soldiers staggering under...the plunder, blankets and leather!" One Captain Oliver at Graham, North Carolina, under

General Joseph E. Johnston, 1807-1891.

Relieved of command of the Army of Tennessee on July 17, 1864, then reinstated on February 25, 1865, with two other departments under him, General Johnston was again engaged in a letter writing frenzy to get supplies for his soldiers, especially shoes.

The fortunes of war and a lot of Yankees were the cause for Joe Johnston's surrender on August 26, 1865, near Durham, North Carolina. His soldiers left for home robbing North Carolina warehouses of clothing and food along the way, but spent the rest of their time on earth with a quick step and wit, "marching light."

threats from a mob of soldiers, emptied his storehouse of 6,300 pairs of pants, 7,000 pounds of leather, 2,100 blankets, 10 coils or rope, and 2,000 yards of jeans cloth.[20]

For weeks, General Johnston had been requesting shoes for his soldiers. Quartermaster Lawton claimed that in March, 7,000 pairs were in shipment, but if they were ever received is unknown. By the end of the month, Johnston was demanding that any shoes remaining in Augusta or Columbus be sent out to him immediately. An official total present of 6,745 men in the Army of Tennessee for March 29, 1865, had 2,298 soldiers reported as barefoot, or very near to it. In the final days of the War, the troops under General Johnston wore the same rags and were as barefooted as their brother soldiers in the Army of Northern Virginia.[21]

For the officers and soldiers, it was time to return to their homes and take up again the lives they had left behind four years earlier. The Yankees gave orders that the former Confederates were not allowed to wear their uniforms in public without removing all military marks, such as buttons or facings. In compliance, they covered their buttons with black cloth, as if in mourning for the cause they served.

It would be a long road back. For most, the remaining years left to them were carried on with the same relish for life and duty that sustained them through four years of hard war. They did it, "marching light."

"They were wearied, earnest looking men, wearing butternut and gray colored clothing and broad-brimmed hats."

— Union soldier at Appomattox

With the arrival of spring in 1865, the Union army began to move. Hood's defeat in Tennessee during the Nashville campaign, and Early's defeat in the Shenandoah Valley by Union General Philip Sheridan, both in late 1864, meant that Grant could be reinforced at Petersburg by another 120,000 men. In an effort to break the siege before the arrival of these reinforcements, Lee chose to attack Union Fort Stedman and drive to City Point, Grant's supply center, and destroy it. The attack on March 25 was initially successful, but a Federal counterattack drove the Confederates back to their entrenchments with heavy losses to the Rebels. A second Confederate defeat at Five Forks on April 1, 1865, and a massive Union attack that pierced their Petersburg defenses on April 2, forced Lee to order a retreat. It was his hope to reach Johnston's forces in southern Virginia and carry on the fight.

Lee's most important consideration for the present was to feed his men. Lee wanted food rations to be sent to Amelia Courthouse, 35 miles south of Richmond, where he had ordered the concentration of his army. On his arrival there he found no rations. By some mix-up, the orders were never received in Richmond by the Commissary Department. It was a disaster, as many of Lee's soldiers had not eaten for days and many deserted the army.

Lee stated in his official report of the surrender at Appomattox that a full 24 hours was expended by the army looking for food in the countryside around Amelia Courthouse. Orders were given to proceed to Farmville where it was hoped rations could be distributed to the men.

Besides food and fatigue, the Union army was pressing Lee's rear. The resulting action fought at Sayler's Creek on April 6, an attempt by the Confederates to protect Lee's wagon trains, was a crushing defeat for the Rebels. Almost all of Ewell's Corps, some 3,000 men, were killed or captured. Both Anderson's and Gordon's Corps were also engaged and forced to retreat under mounting enemy pressure. Ewell blamed his loss on the fact that his men had not slept in four days or eaten in two.[1]

Some rations were finally distributed at Farmville on April 7, but not all could be fed. The close pursuit of the enemy forced the commissary trains to continue their movement toward Appomattox Courthouse. At Appomattox, the army was given a half day to rest and told to prepare to resume their march on April 9.[2]

Lee gave orders for his cavalry and Gordon's Corps to drive forward and push any enemy forces out of the way, then swing around and protect his trains. The resulting skirmishes brought reports of a heavy force of the enemy in his front and on his left flank. With his men on the verge of physical collapse from little sleep and no food, and the Union cavalry threatening his wagon trains and routes of escape, Lee opted to surrender on April

"Taking the Oath of Allegiance."

This illustration shows Confederate soldiers taking their Oath of Allegiance to the Federal government. This sketch is done from life. The Confederates look very ragged and most are in need of shoes. The artist was careful to copy every detail of the prisoners' dress. The high water trousers depicted are interesting. Clothing of all cotton material was issued to the soldiers that winter, and cotton shrinks. Some have caps and others slouch hats.

Confederate Prisoners of Pickett's Division, Battle of Five Forks, April 1, 1865.

This photograph of prisoners from Pickett's Division captured at the Battle of Five Forks depicts the appearance of Robert E. Lee's soldiers in the last months of the War. "Very few of whom had any semblance of uniform. It was a motley group, there being no pretense of uniformity in dress, dirty gray and butternut were the prevailing colors." The men have blanket rolls, canteens, and full haversacks; many have knapsacks.

LOC

Alfred Waud sketches of Confederate Soldiers at Appomatox, Virginia, April 9, 1865.

These sketches from real life, show with some detail the appearance of the Army of Northern Virginia in the last months of the American Civil War. The double haversacks seen on two of the men is interesting, and the diversity in dress and equipments in these sketches is now a matter of record. The duel had been fought — now it was time to go home. The old, *"jacket of gray"* was burned or put away as a souvenir. The old soldiers are gone, but not forgotten.

LOC

9, 1865. In Lee's own words, "I deem this course the best under the circumstances by which we were surrounded."[3] Lee felt his actions justified. "If we had forced our way one day longer it would have been at great sacrifice of life, and at its end I did not see how a surrender could have been avoided."[4]

Descriptions of Lee's soldiers during the Appomattox campaign are numerous. They depict a tired, hungry, and dirty, but resolute group of men who believed they had done their best. The duel had been fought. Both sides had been bloodied, and now it was time to go home. During the surrender ceremony on April 10, 1865, at Appomattox Courthouse, one Union soldier described the exhausted Confederates as, "wearied, earnest looking men, wearing butternut colored and gray clothing and broad-brimmed hats."[5]

One Federal officer remembered the Army of Northern Virginia as a collection of, "dirty, tattered, ranks of soldiers, none of them well clad, and nearly all [the] officers in fatigue dress."[6] Of their weapons, a Federal artilleryman described, "numbers of old Harper's Ferry percussion muskets that had been rifled. I was informed that these had been used by the battalions of reserves which had gone with Lee's main army when Richmond was evacuated, but the standard weapon of the Confederate Infantry appeared to be the Enfield."[7]

Numbers of ex-Confederate soldiers were found making their way home on the Virginia back roads by the Union army. Union soldiers shared their rations with these men, as well as anything else they could supply. One observation made on the Confederates' appearance was, "That very few of whom had any semblance of a uniform but were clad in homespun butternut cloth. It was hard to distinguish betwixt the officers and the privates, as they were all dressed alike."[8] Confederate stragglers picked up during the retreat were said to be, "dirty, crestfallen, haggard, and nearly starved. Nobody would touch one of their garments with a ten foot pole. They are alive with little "graybacks." Besides, they have few garments to throw away. Their destitution is pitiful. Many are barefooted."[9]

Confederate prisoners taken at the Battle of Sayler's Creek, mostly men of Ewell's Corps, were in much better shape than most, and were described as:

> able-bodied and healthy. Many of them had picked up our cast away blankets and overcoats. Nearly all had shoes.... It was a motley group, there being no pretense of uniformity in dress. Dirty gray and butternut were the prevailing colors. Most of them wore old, seedy, slouched hats of brown color. Many were mere boys, and others graybeards.[10]

As to these uniform descriptions, it appears that nothing really changed from the spring of 1862 to April 1865. The same mixed gray and brown clothing, slouch hats, rolled blankets and quilts, poorly shod or barefooted soldiers, and a lot of captured Union clothing, weapons, and equipments, much of it dirty and ragged, seems to run throughout this book. The jacket and pants sewing patterns and cloth used did change over the years, and a lot of imported clothing came through to the armies, but it was apparently never enough to fill all the requisitions. Periods of want and suffering afflicted both the Army of Tennessee and the Army of Northern Virginia, along with times of abundance.

The soldiers of the Army of Northern Virginia, like their brothers in the West, left for home with the belief that they had done their duty, and though defeated in battle, they were not defeated in spirit. The poem, *Old Jacket of Gray* became a symbol of that spirit and still carries with it a nostalgia difficult to describe to those unschooled in the mystique of the Civil War. The only question left is, why no one wrote a poem to the, "Old Jacket of Butternut"?

Confederate Officers 1864

Another Great drawing by Edwin Forbes depicting three Confederate Officers captured in 1864 near Petersburg, Virginia. The first Officer's uniform is regulation. The center figure wears a blouse with two stars on the lapel, and a slouch hat with cord. The far right figure is dressed like a civilian and could be an aide or a private detailed to staff duties, or another officer. By mid-war, a full regulation Confederate Officer's uniform would cost $1,700 in Confederate money. Descriptions of Confederate Officers dressed in privates uniforms or home sewn clothing was the result.

Endnotes

Chapter 1, Part 1
1. *Van Buren* (Arkansas) *Press*, May 1, 1861.
2. *The War of the Rebellion: A Compilation of the Official Records of the Union and Confederate Armies*, 70 vols. in 4 series, (Washington, D.C.: United States Government Printing Office, 1889), Series I., Vol. III, 588, Hereafter cited as *OR*s. T. C. Hindman to L. P. Walker, May 29, 1861.
3. *Montgomery* (Alabama) *Advertiser*, May 6, 1861. Also in Arkansas, Tennessee, and South Carolina newspapers.
4. Eggleston, George A., *A Rebel's Recollections* (Cambridge, NY: Riverside Press, 1875) 12.
5. *Ibid.*, 50.
6. Ford, Marion J., *Life in the C. S. Army*, (New York and Washington: The Neale Publishing Co. 1905) 11.
7. *Richmond* (Virginia) *Enquirer*, October 17, 1861.

Chapter 1, Part 2
1. Todd, Frederick, George Woodbridge, Lee Wallace Jr., and Michael J. McAfee, *American Military Equipage 1851-1872*, (New York: Scribners, 1980) 423-424; *Confederate Chronicles of Tennessee*, Vol. 2, 1987; McClone, J., *Confederate or Imperial Russian? The Design of the Uniform of the Confederate States Army*, 191-194.
2. *Columbus* (Georgia) *Daily Enquirer*, June 6, 1861. Stated: "infantry and cavalry will bear only the number of regiments."
3. General Order No. 9, Uniform and Dress of the Army, Sec. 5.
4. *Ibid.*, Sections 28, 29, 30, 31.
5. *Ibid.*, Sections 1, 51 59.
6. *Ibid.*, Section 19.
7. *Ibid.*, Section 18.
8. Dobbins, Austin C., *Grandfather's Journal, Co. B. 16th Mississippi Infantry Volunteers* (Dayton, OH: Morningside Press, 1988) 10.
9. Stevens, J.W., *Reminiscences of the Civil War* (Hillsboro, TX: Hillsboro Mirror Print, 1902) 8.
10. Russell, William H., *My Civil War Diary*, quoted in Lord, Wise, *Uniforms of the Civil War* (London: A. S. Barnes & Co., 1970) 115-116.
11. *Quincy* (Illinois) *Whig and Republican*, August 10, 1861; Russell Diary.
12. Commanger, Henry S., *The Blue and the Gray* (Indianapolis, IN: Bobbs Merrill, 1950) 64.
13. *Ibid.*, 65.
14. Bevier, R. S., *History of the First and Second Missouri Confederate Missouri Brigades* (St. Louis, MO: Bryan, Brand & Co. 1879) 75.
15. Hancock, Enoch, 3rd Tennessee Infantry, A.C. No. 1528. 9-19. Tennessee State Archives, Special Collections.

Chapter 1, Part 3
1. *OR*, Series IV, Vol. 1, 506; Fayetteville, Tennessee Committee to L.P. Walker, July 29, 1861.
2. *Ibid.*, 507.
3. *Ibid.*, 534. L.P. Walker, Secretary of War, to the Governors of Alabama, Arkansas, Florida, Georgia, Mississippi, North Carolina, South Carolina, Tennessee, Texas, and Virginia.
4. *Ibid.*, 537-38. John Lechter, Governor of Virginia, to L.P. Walker, Secretary of War, August 9, 1861.
5. *Ibid.*, 694. Joseph E. Brown, Governor of Georgia, to Judah P. Benjamin, Acting Secretary of War, October 19, 1861. Brown was concerned that under the Commutation Law, "in case any State shall furnish to its troops such clothing, are they to follow the [uniform regulations] of the Department?"
6. *Ibid.* Considering the type of military clothing needed under the regulations and the scarcity of the proper materials in the Southern marketplace, Benjamin's decision was the only one he could make under the circumstances.
7. Jones, J. B. *A Rebel War Clerk's Diary*, Vol.1, (Philadelphia: J. B. Lippincott Co., 1866) 84.
8. *Texas Republican*, Marshall, Texas, October 12, 1861.
9. *Ibid*.
10. *Houston Tri-weekly Telegraph*, Texas, October 20, 1861.
11. *Texas Republican*, December 7, 1861. Letter dated November, 1861, Peterson, Kentucky.
12. *Ibid.* October 29, 1861.
13. *Ibid*.
14. *Columbus Daily Enquirer*, Georgia. September 10, 1861.
15. *Memphis* (Tennessee) *Appeal*, November 13, 1861.
16. *Columbus* (Georgia) *Daily Enquirer*, February 15, 1862.
17. *Ibid*.
18. *San Antonio* (Texas) *Weekly Herald*, November 9, 1861.
19. *Clarksville* (Tennessee) *Chronicle*, August 30, 1861.
20. *Fayetteville* (Tennessee) *Observer*, October 8, 1861.
21. *Ibid*.
22. *San Antonio Herald*, November 2, 1861.
23. Goff, Richard, D., *Confederate Supply*, (Durham: NC. 1969) 49.

Chapter 1, Part 4
1. *OR*, Series IV, Vol. 1, 229, General Order No. 8. S. Cooper, Adjutant and Inspector General.
2. Soldier's Letter, *Fayetteville* (Tennessee) *Observer*, May 2, 1861.
3. *OR*, Series IV, Vol. 1, 307, L. P. Walker to Governor Joseph E. Brown, May 8, 1861.
4. *OR*, Series IV, 487-489, L. P. Walker to Jefferson Davis, Letter dated July 24, 1861.
5. *Ibid*.
6. Todd, 426.
7. Goff, 18.
8. *Ibid*.
9. *New York Herald*, November 12, 1861.
10. Jones, T., *Hood's Texas Brigade: A Compendium* (Hillsboro, TX: Hill Junior College Press, 1977).
11. *New York Herald*, August 12, 1861.
12. *Memphis Appeal*, October 17, 1861.
13. *Ibid*.
14. *OR*, Series IV, Vol. 1, 688. A.C. Myers, Acting Quartermaster-General to Hon. J. P. Benjamin.
15. *OR*, Series IV, Vol. 1, 701. A.B. Moore, Governor of Alabama, to the Alabama State House, October 28, 1861.
16. Hill, Mary S., *A British Subject's Recollections of the Confederacy* (Baltimore: Turnball Bros. 1875) August 2, 1861.
17. *Ibid*.

18. *OR*, Series IV, Vol. 1, 884, Report of a Mr. Wall, January 29, 1862.
19. *Ibid.*

Chapter 1, Part 5
1. *New York Herald*, October 30, 1861. The same reporter mentioned how he saw, "gray uniformed fellows from Louisiana" at the Depot in Columbus, Kentucky, probably the 11th Louisiana Infantry.
2. *Belvidere* (Illinois) *Standard*, November 15, 1861. From insert that appeared in the Missouri Republican, St.Louis, Missouri.
3. *Baton Rouge* (Louisiana) *Gazette*, November 8, 1861. Letter dated October 28, 1861.
4. *Ibid.*
5. *Champaign* (Illinois) *Gazette*, November 3, 1861. Soldier's letter.
6. Smith, H. I., *History of the 7th Iowa Veteran Volunteer Infantry* (Mason City, IA: 1903), 22.
7. OR, Series I, Vol. 3, 688. A. S. Johnston to Mississippi Gov. John Pettus November 21, 1861.
8. *Ibid.*, 826. L. Polk to A. S. Johnston.
9. *Freeport* (Illinois) *Weekly Press*, January 1, 1862.
10. OR, Series I, Vol. 3, 694. M. Lovell, Cmd'g, Dept. No. 1 in New Orleans, to A. S. Johnston, November 23, 1861.
11. Miller, Thomas F., 29th Illnois Infantry, letter dated February 10, 1862. Illnois State Historical Society special collections vault; *Waukegan* (Illinois) *Weekly Gazette*, February 15, 1862, soldier's letter from Fort Henry.
12. *Memphis* (Tennessee) *Appeal*, February 12, 1862. From an insert that originally appeared in the *Chicago Tribune*.
13. *Bloomington* (Illinois) *Pantagraph*, February 25, 1862, soldier's letter.
14. *Ibid.*, February 21, 1862.
15. *Ottawa* (Illinois) *Free Trader*, March 8, 1862.
16. *Carlyle* (Illinois) *Weekly Reveille*, February 23, 1862.
17. Bearss, E. C., "Unconditional Surrender, the Fall of Fort Donelson," Reprint, Tennessee Historical Quarterly. March 1962, 36-37.
18. *Ibid.*, 37.
19. *Louisville* (Kentucky) *Journal*, n.d., February, 1862.
20. Fenton, James, Co. K., 19th Illinois Infantry, diary entry April 5, 1862, Chicago Historical Society, Special Collections.
21. McMorries, E. Y., *History of the First Alabama Infantry, C.S.A.*, (Montgomery, AL: Brown Printing, 1904) 23.
22. Stillwell, Leander, *The Story of the Common Soldier of the Civil War* (Kansas City, MO: Franklin Hudson Publishing Co.,1920) 39.
23. Sword, Wiley, *Shiloh, Bloody April*, (Dayton, OH: Morningside Bookshop, 1983) 146.
24. *Ottawa* (Illinois) *Free Trader*, April 18, 1862. Soldier's letter, Ottawa Light Artillery.
25. Harrison, Jon. *The Rebel Index*, Vol. X, No. 8.
26. Sword, Wiley, *Shiloh, Bloody April*, p. 317-318.
27. *Waukegan* (Illinois) *Weekly Gazette*, April 23, 1862.
28. Duncan, Thomas D., *Forrest's Command Mississippi Cavalry*. (Nashville, TN: McQuiddy Printing, 1922) 57.
29. Letters, 29th Ohio Infantry. Private collection.
30. *Rushville* (Illinois) *Citizen*, October 10, 1862.
31. *Woodstock* (Illinois) *Sentinel*, Letter, 95th Illinois Infantry, December 15, 1862.

Chapter 1, Part 6
1. *Clarksville* (Tennessee) *Chronicle*, November 22, 1861.
2. *Ibid.*, October 15, 1861.
3. *Bloomington* (Illinois) *Pantagraph*, February 10, 1862. Soldier's letter.
4. Miller, F., 8th Illinois Infantry. Special Collections, Illinois State Historical Society.
5. Forrest, Nathan B., Special Report [Nashville Panic] A. C. 824, Tennessee State Library.
6. *Ibid.*
7. *Ibid.*
8. Allen, Henry A., *11th Illinois Cavalry*. Special Collections, Illinois State Historical Society.
9. *Rushville* (Illinois) *Citizen*, May 22, 1862.
10. *Ibid.* Letter of A.G. Meacham to his wife, Reprint.
11. *Warren* (Illinois) *Independent*, May 13, 1862, Soldier's letter.
12. *Carlinville* (Illinois) *Free Democrat*, June 10, 1862. Soldier's letter, 32nd Illinois Infantry.
13. OR, Series IV, Vol. 1, 1042, A. C. Myers to G. W. Randolph, April 2, 1862.
14. *Ibid.*
15. *Missouri Republican*, October 8, 1862.
16. *Ibid.*
17. *Galveston* (Texas) *News*, December 12, 1862.
18. Bevier, 166.
19. Hall, Winchester, *The Story of the 26th Louisiana Infantry in the Service of the Confederate States* (Private printed, n.d.) 24. Wisconsin State Historical Society Collections.
20. Womack, James J., *A Civil War Diary* (McMinville, TN: Womack Printing Co. 1961) 68. 16th Tennessee Infantry, diary entry of October 28, 1862.
21. *Augusta* (Georgia) *Constitutionalist*, March 3, 1863.
22. *Ibid.*, February 21, 1863.
23. Jones, 203.

Chapter 1, Part 7
1. Manigault, Arthur M., *The Civil War Narrative of Arthur Middleton Manigault*, R. Lockwood Tower, ed. (Columbia, SC: USC Press, 1983) 51.
2. *Columbus* (Georgia) *Daily Enquirer*, July 12, 1861.
3. *The Rebel Index*, Vol. X. No. 8, Harrison, John, "The Color of Confederate Uniforms."
4. Maigault, 51.
5. Letters from the 28th Alabama, Private collection.
6. *Ibid.*
7. *Camp Chase Gazette*, 1981. Confederate diary reprint, courtesy Phil Katcher notes and Camp Chase Gazette.
8. *Atlanta* (Georgia) *Intelligencier*, February 20, 1863.

Chapter 1, Part 8
1. Wheeler, Richard, *Sword Over Richmond* (New York, NY: Fairfax Press, 1989) 144. Found in the *Boston Journal*.
2. Lord, Francis and Arthur Wise, *Uniforms of the Civil War*, 120, quoted from *History of the Fortieth Regiment New York Volunteers*.
3. *Ibid.*, 120.
4. *The Rebel Index*, Vol. X, No. 8, Harrison, John, "The Color of Confederate Uniforms," as quoted by Townsend, *Rustics in Rebellion*.
5. Goss, W. L., "Recollections of a Private," *The Century Illustrated Monthly Magazine*, Vol. 29, 1884-1885, 65.
6. Commanger, 175.
7. Cooke, John Esten, *The Life of Jackson* (C. B. Richardson:1863) 280.

8. Chamberlayne, Churchill. *Ham Chamberlayne—Virginian: Letters and Papers of an Artillery Officer*. (Richmond: 1932) 99.
9. *Harper's Weekly Magazine*.
10. Durkin, Joseph T., ed., *John Dooley, Confederate Soldier, His War Journal* (Washington, DC: Georgetown University Press, 1945) 62.
11. Williams, H. D., "The Glory of War: Johnny Reb and the Antietam Campaign," *Civil War Quarterly*, Vol. IX, 15.
12. Krick, Robert, "The Army of Northern Virginia in September, 1862," *Essays on the 1862 Maryland Campaign*, Gary W. Gallagher, ed.,. 41.
13. Von Borcke, Heros, *Memoirs of the Confederate War for Independence* (New York:1938) 230.
14. Antietam notes — source unknown.
15. Thompson, D. L. "With Burnside at Antietam," *Battles and Leaders*, 662.
16. Antietam notes — source unknown.
17. Thompson, D. L. "In the Ranks to Antietam," *Battles and Leaders*, 558.
18. *Constitutionalist*, March 3, 1863.
19. *Columbus* (Georgia) *Daily Enquirer*, October 4, 1862.
20. *Ibid*., November 15, 1861.
21. *Ibid*., September 3, 1861.
22. *Ibid*., March 24, 1862.
23. *Constitutionalist*, July 6, 1862.
24. Worsham, J.H.,*One of Jackson's Foot Cavalry* (New York: The Neale Publishing Co. 1912) 74. 25   McCarthy.
26. *Constitutionalist*, December, 1862.
27. *Ibid*.
28. *Ibid*., January 17, 1863.

Chapter 2, Part 1
1. *OR*, Series IV, Vol. 2, General Orders No. 100, 229-230, S. Cooper, Adj. and Inspector General.
2. *Ibid*. Article XIV, 231.
3. Caldwell, J.F.J., *The History of a Brigade of South Carolinians* (Philadelphia: 1866) 70.
4. *Ibid*. 70.
5. *Southern Confederacy*, Virginia, March 19, 1863, letter signed "Cavalier."
6. Hale, L. and S. Phillips, *History of the Forty-Ninth Virginia Infantry* (Lanham, MD: S.S. Phillips and Assoc., 1981) 71.
7. *Ibid*., 71.
8. Meyers, Thomas R., Co. F. 41st Tennessee Infantry, Tennessee State Library, A.C. No. 1309, 5.
9. Shotwell, R.A., "Three Years in Battle: The Papers of Robert Abbott Shotwell," *The Blue and the Gray* (Commanger) 314-316.
10. Manigault, 255. It is interesting to note that in September 1862, the Army of Tennessee under Bragg was given preferential treatment over the Army of Northern Virginia!
11. *Southern Confederacy*, March 20, 1863.
12. *Ibid*.
13. *Daily Constitutionalist*, December 15, 1862.
14. Goff, 69-71; *OR*, Series IV, Vol. VII, 691.
15. *OR*, Series IV, Vol. 2, Proclamation of Z. B. Vance, Governor of North Carolina, Nov. 26, 1862, 214.

Chapter 2, Part 2
1. Drickamer, Les and Karen, *Harper's Ferry on the Border: North and South with "Ramblin Jour"* (Shippensburg, PA: White Mane, 1987) 111-113.
2. *Berkshire* (Massachusetts) *County Eagle*, June 25, 1863.
3. Bull, Rice C., *Soldiering: The Civil War Diary of Rice C. Bull*, (San Rafael, CA. Presidio Press, 1977) 60.
4. Brainard, *Campaigns of the 146th Regiment Infantry* (New York: 1915) 95. Mike McAfee uniform notes.
5. Fremantle, J.A. L. *Fremantle Diary* (London, 1956) 180.
6. Shotwell, 314-316.
7. Early, J.A., *Narrative of the War Between the States* (J. B. Lippincott Co., 1912) 238.
8. *Ibid*., 238.
9. Dooley, J., *John Dooley, Confederate Soldier*, ed., J.T. Durkin, (South Bend, IN: 1963) 100.
10. Catton, B., *Bruce Catton's America* (New York: Promontory Press, 1993) 98-99.
11. Goss, 199.
12. *Fremantle Diary*, *Ibid*., 191. Confederate QM records show the Texas Brigade received new clothing just prior to the Gettysburg battle, on June 30 to be exact. R.G. 109, Roll 255, 288, 293.
13. *Ibid*., 186.
14. Forbes, E., *An Artist's Story of the Great War* (Fords Howard Holbrook, 1899) 274.
15. Worsham, 173.

Chapter 2, Part 3
1. *OR*, Series IV, Vol. 2, Circular. Richmond, March 24, 1863.
2. *Constitutionalist*, February 14, 1863.
3. Todd Notes, Courtesy Brown University. Peter Harrington, Archivist.
4. *Wilmington* (North Carolina) *Daily Journal*, October 1, 1864.
5. Todd Notes, Courtesy Brown University. Peter Harrington, Archivist.
6. *Wilmington* (North Carolina) *Daily Journal*, June 6, 1864.
7. *Constitutionalist*, July 7, 1862.
8. *Columbus* (Georgia) *Weekly Sun*, April 24, 1863.
9. *OR*, Series I, Vol. 23, Part II, Exhibit E, April 4,1863, Maj. V. K. Stevenson to Col. Wm. Preston.
10. *Virginia Daily Examiner*, October 16, 1861.
11. *Richmond* (Virginia) *Enquirer*.
12. Rauscher, Frank, *Music on the March: a History of the 114th Pennsylvania*, 134. Courtesy of Mike McAfee.
13. Hale, Laura, *Phillips Stanley, History of the 49th Virginia*, 134.
14. Haskell, *1st South Carolina Volunteers, Alexander Cheves Haskell, Portrait of a Man*, 65; Mixom, Frank M., *1st South Carolina Volunteers Reminiscences of a Private*, 1910. 41.
15. Ives, Washington, *Civil War Journal and Letters*. Jim R. Cabaniss, ed. (1987) 47, 59.

Chapter 2, Part 4
1. *Southern Confederacy*, Atlanta, Georgia. January 21, 1863.
2. *Ibid*.
3. *Ibid*., January 13, 1863. Soldier's letter.
4. *Ibid*.
5. Matthews, W.E., Memoirs, 33rd Alabama Infantry, Alabama State Historical by permission, 21.
6. *OR*, Series I., Vol 20, Part II, Correspondence, 155
7. *Ibid*., 181.
8. *OR*, Series I., Vo. 20, Part I. Report of Brigadier-General A. P. Stewart, January 5, 1863, 726.
9. *Schyler Citizen*, January 28, 1863.
10. Matthews, 22.
11. Key, Thomas K. *Two Soldiers*, Entry for December 10,1863 (NC: Chapel Hill Press, 1938) 12.

12. Worsham, 106-107.
13. Riley, Franklin, *Grandfather's Journal*, 133.
14. Nichols, G. W., *A Soldier's Story of his Regiment, 61st Georgia*, Bristoe Station, October, 1863, (Jesup & George, 1907) 133.
15. *Richmond Daily Dispatch*, n.d.
16. Eddy, Richard, *History of the 60th N.Y. Infantry* (Philadelphia, PA: 1864) 139.
17. Key, Thomas J., *Two Soldiers*, (NC: Chapel Hill Press, 1938) entry December 10, 1863.
18. Wiley, B.I., *The Life of Johnny Reb* (Baton Rouge, LA: LSU Press, 1978) 115.
19. Brown, D.A., *The Bold Cavaliers: Morgan's 2nd Kentucky Cavalry Raiders* (Philadelphia, PA: J. B. Lippincott, 1959) 140.
20. Ives, W., *Civil War Journal and Letters*, Letter dated 12/3/63, 55.

Chapter 2, Part 5
1. *OR*, Series I, Vol. 23, Part II. Col. Wm. Preston Johnston to President J.C. Davis, April 15, 1863, 757.
2. *Ibid.*, 759.
3. Fremantle, Arthur M., *Fremantle Diary*, Walter Lord, ed. (London: 1956) 124.
4. *Ibid.*
5. *Ibid.*
6. *OR*, Series I., Vol. 23, Part II, 758.
7. *Ibid.*, 763.
8. *Ibid.*, 758.
9. Dickert, Augustus, *History of Kershaw's Brigade*, 1899, 268.
10. Tucker, Glenn, *Chickamauga: Bloody Battle in the West*, (NY: Bobb Merrill Co., 1961) 172.
11. Sorrell, Moxley, *Recollections of a Confederate Staff Officer* (Neale: 1905).
12. Ives, Washington, *Civil War Journal and Letters*, 48.
13. Collins, R. N., *Unwritten Chapters of the War Between the States* (St. Louis, MO: Nixon-Jones Printing Co., 1893) 164.
14. *Ibid.*
15. Matthews, 29.

Chapter 2, Part 6
1. Harris, John W., Harris Black Book, Letter September 22, 1863. Memoirs and Letters, A.C. No. 206, Tennessee Historical Society.
2. *OR*, Vol. XXXII, Pt. 1, 651-667.
3. Report of the Special Committee on the Pay and Clothing of the Army. Confederate House of Representatives, February 11, 1865, 3.
4. *OR*, Series IV, Vol. 3, p. 1040. Quartermaster Lawton report to Hon. Mr. Miller, Chairman, Special Committee, January 27, 1865.
5. Courtesy Mike McAfee. Notes from the History of the 54th Massachusetts.
6. *Wilmington* (North Carolina) *Daily Journal*, April 3, 1863. According to Les Jensen, authority on Confederate uniforms, Confederate officers were allowed to disregard cuff laces due to the expense and trouble of procuring them in the field, as early as 1862.

Chapter 2, Part 7
1. *Keithsburg* (Illinois) *Observer*, January 1, 1864.
2. *Ibid.*, December 10, 1863.
3. Matthews, 32.
4. *OR*, Series I, Vol. 52, Part II. J.C. Ives, aide-de-camp to Jefferson Davis, 574.
5. Johnston, Joseph E., *Narratives of Military Operations During the Civil War*, (New York: D. Appleton & Co., 1874) 268.
6. *Ibid.*, 279.
7. *Galveston* (Texas) *Tri-weekly News*, February 24, 1864. Letter from an unknown soldier.

Chapter 2, Part 8
1. *OR*, Series IV, Vol. V. 2, Quartermaster Lawton to Colin McRae, 872.
2. *OR*, Series I., Vol. 52, Quartermaster Lawton to Jefferson Davis, 615.
3. *OR*, Series I., Vol. 29, Part II, Quartermaster Lawton to Lee, 784.
4. *OR*, Series I., Vol. 30, Part IV. F.W. Dillard to Maj. A. M. Barbour, Chief Quartermaster of Gen. Johnston, September 23, 1863, 730.
5. *Ibid.*, 686.
6. *Ibid.*, 730.
7. *OR*, Series I., Vol. 52, Part II, Quartermaster Lawton to G.W.C. Lee, January 9, 1864, p. 615.
8. *Ibid.*
9. Courtesy Bob Huntoon notes. Large numbers of North Carolina buttons have been dug in the Dalton, Georgia area. They were cut off and replaced with either Confederate "I" buttons or whatever was issued with the owner's old jacket.

Chapter 2, Part 9
1. *OR*, Series I, Vol. 31, Brigadier General Micah Jenkins, enclosure, 470.
2. *Ibid.*, Report of Captain Frank Potts, Assistant Quartermaster C. S. Army, 476.
3. *Ibid.*, 476- 477.
4. *Ibid.*, 477.
5. *Battles and Leaders*, "Longstreet at Knoxville" by Gen. E. P. Alexander. See also *OR*, Series I, Vol. 31, Part I, E. P. Alexander Report, 480.
6. Longstreet, James L., *From Manassas to Appomattox*, 526.
7. Sorrell, Moxley, *Recollections of a Confederate Staff Officer*.
8. *Battles and Leaders*, 750.
9. Longstreet, 521.
10. *Ibid.*, 525. See also Goff, *Confederate Supply*, 147.
11. *OR*, Series I., Vol. 32. Lt. Colonel Sorrel to Col. Ira Foster, March 22, 1864, 666-667.

Chapter 2, Part 10
1. *OR*, Series I, Part II, Vol. 29, Lee to Q.M.G. Lawton, October 19, 1863, 794.
2. *Ibid.*, Lee to Secretary of War Seddon, October 23, 1863, 800.
3. *Ibid.*, Lee to Seddon, 830. Lee reports the receipt of some shoes, but remarks "All should be well shod and clothed in such weather."
4. *Ibid.*, Seddon to Lee, 835. Seddon apologizes to Lee that the "supplies sent by railroad had not been forwarded as promptly as [Q.M.G. Lawton] had expected."
5. Ibid., 835.
6. Letter, Courtesy of Mr. Dennis Kelly, Kennesaw Mountain National Battlefield Park Collection.
7. Special Collections, Tennessee State Archives, A.C. No. 1379. Manuscript section, Letter Dalton, April 20, 1864.

8. Special Collections, Tennessee State Archives, A.C. No. 1392.
9. *OR*, Series I, Vol. 29, Part III, Lee to Seddon, November 19, 1863, 837. See also Lee to Northrop, 844.
10. *Ibid.*, 889-890.
11. *Ibid.*, 890.
12. Howard, McHenry, *Recollections of a Maryland Confederate Soldier and Staff Officer Under Johnston, Jackson & Lee* (Baltimore, MD: 1914) 248-251.
13. Dobbins, A., *Grandfather's Journal*, 181.
14. Pickett Papers, Reel 65, MSS 13744, Tennessee State Archives.
15. Caldwell, J.F.J., *This History of a Brigade of South Carolinians*, 122.
16. *Columbus (Georgia) Daily Enquirer*. Issue, November 15, 1863, Private James H. Tigner, 12th La. Infantry.

Chapter 2, Part 11
1. *OR*, Series IV, Vol 2, 1007-1008, Report to Jefferson Davis from Seddon, 11/26/63.
2. *Ibid.*, 382-383.
3. *OR*, Series IV., Vol. 3, 958.
4. *Ibid.*
5. Yearns and Barrett, *North Carolina Civil War Documentary* (Chapel Hill, NC: University of North Carolina Press, 1980) 70.
6. *Ibid.*, 70.
7. *Ibid.*, 77.

Chapter 3, Part 1
1. *OR*, Series IV, Vol. 3, p. 210-211, Lawton to Mr. Thomas Sharp, March 12, 1864.
2. *Ibid.* p. 288, Lawton to R. P. Waller, Nassau, April 12, 1864.
3. *Ibid.* p. 526, C. J. McRae to Seddon, July 4, 1864.
4. See also, *Military Collector and Historian Journal*, Vol. XLI, No. 4, Winter 1989, Jensen, L. D., *A Survey of Confederate Central General Issue Jackets, Part II*.
5. *OR*, Series IV, Vol. 3, p. 556-557, Lawton to Seddon, July 26, 1864.
6. *Ibid.*
7. *Ibid.* p. 671-672, Governor Vance to Seddon, Sept. 19, 1864.
8. *Ibid.* p. 690-692, Lawton to Seddon, Sept. 28, 1864.
9. *OR*, Series IV, Vol. 3, p. 674, Lawton to J. P. Ferguson, London, Sept. 21, 1864.
10. Pamphlet, Memorandum of Resources of Department Clothing, Comp. Equip. and Miscellaneous Store No. 2.
11. *Ibid.*
12. See also, *OR*, Series IV, Vol. 3, p. 1039-1040, Lawton to Miller, Chairman Special Committee, Jan. 27, 1865.
13. Cross, Memorandum, no page. [See footnote 12.]
14. Miller, S. A., *Report, Special Committee on the pay and Clothing of the Army*, p.5, Feb. 11, 1865.

Chapter 3, Part 2
1. Manigault, 178.
2. R.G. 109, C.S.R., Roll 299, National Archives Microfilm.
3. Courtesy Phil Katcher Notes — source unknown.

Chapter 3, Part 3
1. *OR*, Series IV, Vol. 3, 1094, Secretary of War John C. Breckenridge to President Jefferson Davis, February 18, 1865.
2. *OR*, Series IV, Vol. 3, 1088. Major A.H. Cole to Q.M.G. Lawton, February 1, 1865.
3. *Ibid.*, 1088.
4. *Ibid.*, 1090. Major Wm. B.B. Cross to Secretary of War, John C. Breckenridge, February 17, 1865.
5. *Ibid.*, 1032. Major B.P. Noland to R.W. Noland, January 23, 1865.
6. *Ibid.*, 1091, Lt. Col. F.W. Sims to Lawton, February 10, 1865.
7. *Ibid.*, 1092.
8. *Ibid.*, 1093, 1098. Lawton to Breckinridge, February 16, 1865.
9. *Ibid.*, 1094.
10. *Ibid.*, 1155, An Act to raise coin for the purpose of furnishing necessary supplies to the army, March 17, 1865.
11. Goff, 240-241.
12. Alexander, 504.

Chapter 3, Part 4
1. Wiley, Bell I., *Life of Johnny Reb*, (Indianapolis, IN: 1943) Letter, Sebron Sneed to his wife, June 7, 1864.
2. *OR*, Series IV, Vol. 3, 1041. Lawton to Miller, Committee Chairman, January 27, 1865.
3. Daniel, Larry J., *Cannoneers in Gray*, Found in AGIR Artillery Inspection, August 18, 1864; *OR*, XXXVIII, Part I, 828; *OR*, Part 3, 904-905.
4. Smith, Aaron, *On Wheels and How I Came There, Co. K. 14th Ill. Inf.* (Cincinnati, OH: 1892) 194-195.
5. *Ibid.*, 200.
6. *Ibid.*, 201.
7. *Wilmington (North Carolina) Daily Journal*, 10/27/64.
8. *Ibid.*
9. *OR*, Series I, Vol 45, Part 1, 733-739.
10. Dunlap, Samuel B., Diary, October 28 - Nov. 1, 1864, State Historical Society of Missouri.
11. Matthews, W. E., 33rd Alabama, Diary.
12. Houghton, W., 23rd Michigan, Wiley Sword Notes.
13. *Ibid.*
14. Weaver, Adam J., 104th Ohio, Wiley Sword Notes.
15. Rogers, Hobart, 42nd Illinois Diary, Illinois State Historical Society.
16. Maxwell, George, *History Lumsden's Battery* (Tuscaloosa, AL: 1905) 60.
17. *OR*, Series I. Vol. 45. Part 1, 733-739
18. Lumsdens, 63.
19. Rennolds, E. H., *A History of the Henry County Commands* (Jacksonville, FL: Sun Publishing, 1904) 291.
20. *OR*, Series I, Vol. 45; Ibid.
21. *Ibid.*

Chapter 3, Part 5
1. *Battles and Leaders*, From Ewell's Official Report, 721.
2. *Ibid.*, 724.
3. *Ibid.*
4. *Ibid.*
5. Goss, 353.
6. Calkins, 56, with permission.
7. *Ibid.*, 40-41.
8. *Ibid.*, 73.
9. *Ibid.*
10. *Ibid.*, 188.

THOMAS PUBLICATIONS publishes books about the American Colonial era, the Revolutionary War, the Civil War, and other important topics. For a complete list of titles, please visit our website at:

www.thomaspublications.com

Or write to:

THOMAS PUBLICATIONS
P.O. Box 3031
Gettysburg, Pa. 17325